Theodore Wright

Queensland horticulturist and gardeners guide

with hints to new-comers

Theodore Wright

Queensland horticulturist and gardeners guide
with hints to new-comers

ISBN/EAN: 9783742848055

Manufactured in Europe, USA, Canada, Australia, Japa

Cover: Foto ©Lupo / pixelio.de

Manufactured and distributed by brebook publishing software (www.brebook.com)

Theodore Wright

Queensland horticulturist and gardeners guide

THE QUEENSLAND HORTICULTURIST

AND

GARDENER'S GUIDE,

BY T. WRIGHT;

ALSO,

HINTS TO NEW-COMERS,

BY P. FLETCHER.

PRICE THREE SHILLINGS.

BRISBANE:
JAMES C. BEAL, GOVERNMENT PRINTER, WILLIAM STREET.

1886.

PREFACE.

ENCOURAGED by the prompt sale of my "Fruit Cultivation in Queensland," a second edition of which is now demanded, I have put together a goodly number of hints and instructions written at odd times for the *Queenslander*, to assist our gardening friends in their trying and oftimes perplexing avocations. Having had a number of years' experience in this sunny clime, and also a very successful one, I am thereby qualified by my own experience to render valuable assistance to others; and I am satisfied that those who are contented to follow the directions furnished herein will make very few mistakes or failures. Experience gathered in other climes will not be found applicable here, and when for a few shillings a person may be put upon the right track at once, the outlay is infinitely better than a waste of time and labour. This is not a complete guide on gardening matters, but it covers very much of the ground; and the two Prize Essays which mainly form the work—"Fruit Cultivation in Queensland" and "Orange Culture"—are honestly worth more than the price.

The Author not only understands, but is an enthusiast in, gardening matters, and from a desire to magnify his calling and make it honourable, profitable, and satisfactory, has given thus his convictions and experience that others may have the free use of his intelligence. In the hope that the book will supply a want, and do honest and useful work, it is sent forth by the Author.

THEODORE WRIGHT.

18th January, 1886.

CONTENTS.

FRUITS ADAPTED TO QUEENSLAND—

	PAGE.
Introductory	1
Suitable Soil for the Work	3
Method of Cultivation	6
Draining Land	8
Planting the Trees	10
Pruning for Fruit	15
Grape Culture	18
Picking and Packing	19
Marketable Value	21
Coffee	22
Coffee-Tea	23

ORANGE CULTURE—

Introductory	24
Interviewing Dame Nature	25
Is the Orange-tree a Surface Rooter?	26
Preparing the Land—	
Draining	27
Trenching	29
Shelter and Mulch	31
Orange or Lemon Stocks	32
Proper Planting Distance	33
Pruning the Trees	35
Manuring	37
Orange Pests	38
The Citrus Family	39

HINTS TO NEW-COMERS—

Introductory	42
Tent Life	51
Bark Huts	55
Tree-falling and Tools	60
Splitting Shingles	64
Slab Huts	68
Hut Furniture	77

CONTENTS.

USEFUL GARDENING OPERATIONS—

	PAGE.
Plant Propagation...	84
Striking Cuttings ...	84
Budding ...	88
Layering	89
Grafting ...	90
Pruning	93
Receipt for Grafting Wax	97
Bush-houses ...	97

FLOWER CULTURE — 100

HINTS ON POULTRY KEEPING — 103

FIELD AND GARDEN CALENDAR—

January	107
February	109
March	112
April	115
May	117
June	120
July	123
August	126
September	130
October	132
November	135
December	137

FRUITS ADAPTED TO QUEENSLAND.

INTRODUCTORY.

FRUIT fills an important part in the economy of our nature, and should be regarded by all as an essential article of diet. In a tropical country like this it should be both plentiful and cheap, so that all classes, whatever their means, might indulge in it without stint. Unfortunately this is not the case; and yet possibly no country in the world enjoys a wider range of productiveness in this particular. As yet the fruit industry is in its infancy in Queensland. Numerous experiments have been tried in growing fruit over most of the territory, and results so far justify the expectation that at no distant date she must become a great fruit-producing country; and anything like a successful attempt to help it forward will by the many be highly appreciated.

The immense variety of fruits capable of being grown successfully in this highly favoured land is almost incredible to the uninitiated. The elevated lands in the interior are well adapted for growing nearly all the fruits of the temperate zone. On the Darling Downs and from thence to Stanthorpe, and also on the Peak Downs and other places similarly located, the apple, pear, quince, plum, cherry, peach, apricot, nectarine, almond, olive, passion-fruit, grape, fig, pomegranate, persimmon (or Chinese date plum), medlar, mulberry, loquat, chestnut, walnut, filbert, raspberry, blackberry, elderberry, strawberry, and even the gooseberry and the red, white, and black currants, may be successfully fruited. They will not all do equally well, and some of them—especially gooseberries, currants, and cherries—will only be found profitable in a few favoured localities; still, the great variety left to choose from, and most of which with proper culture and care will do well, are quite sufficient to suit all tastes and supply the markets. The districts mentioned are also adapted for the orange, lemon, and shaddock, which they may grow in common with all other parts of the colony; but for the varieties before mentioned these districts are specially adapted.

In higher latitudes and on the coast south of the tropic of Capricorn such fruits as the guava, mango, banana, pine-apple, orange, lemon, citron, shaddock, lime, passion-fruit, granadilla, custard-apple, papau, date, rose-apple, longan, litchee, wampee, and the alligator pear may be grown; and in the tropical north, also to a limited extent farther south, close along the coast and in sheltered localities, the jack-fruit, mangosteen, durion, bread-fruit, and the cocoanut. wine and date palms will find a home and flourish. One variety of the

B

mangosteen—the Cochin gorke—will thrive in a lower temperature than others of that fruit; and the durion and the bread-fruit are both particularly tender and will not endure severe cold, much less frost; so that the limit of their probable cultivation in this colony is very small. In the decidedly tropical portions of the colony the fruits of the temperate zone will prove to a great extent out of place, and yet it would be advisable to plant them in limited quantities in every large collection until it is ascertained with certainty what can and what cannot be grown profitably. Nearly all the valuable fruits indigenous to the tropics everywhere will in some portion of the colony be grown some day; at present, however, many of them are not to be had, and the work already done by our Acclimatisation Society is worthy of being continued to the end.

In Queensland, therefore, the fruit-grower has scope hardly to be found in any other portion of the globe, and although the pioneers of this industry may spend a good deal of time and money to very little purpose while acquiring the experience needful to success, eventually the raising of fruit will be an industry of considerable importance to the State; and with the prospect of a short passage to Europe by fast steamers, and the fitting-up therein of refrigerating chambers, or the application of some one of the many chemical compounds now coming into notice as antiseptics, there is every probability, and that not at all remote, that Queensland will yet successfully compete with other fruit-growing countries in the supply of the European markets.

The great principles which underlie success in this industry are the same everywhere; but there are peculiar circumstances of climate and soil in this country which call for special treatment, and these are by the many totally ignored to the consequent failure of their labour and expenditure.

There is no cultural industry of more promise than the cultivation of fruit in one or other of its many branches. It is not a work for the novice or the easy-going and careless to enter upon, nevertheless; for while the possibilities of the soil and climate are what is stated, good results will never be achieved without a fair share of knowledge and skill in the first place, and the utmost care and vigilance always in contending against the many ills that fruit in Queensland is heir to. The man who loves his ease, and cannot put up with frequent crosses and disappointments, need not expect to be among the successful orchardists anywhere, least of all in this colony. It is necessary to say this much to prevent men disqualified by Nature for the work entering upon it to their own and the colony's injury; at the same time, where men have a taste for it, with the necessary skill and experience, and can patiently bear up against occasional disappointments while battling manfully with difficulties, there is sufficient reason for them to undertake it with energy and spirit, for to such there is money in it. Enthusiasm is an important qualification for the industry, for with it and plenty of energy a success may be achieved **with but little knowledge of the details of the work to begin with.**

SUITABLE SOIL FOR THE WORK.

It is a matter of very great importance in fruit-growing to select land suitable for the purpose. A little thought will serve to make this clear. For instance, we will suppose a man commences to lay out a piece of land for an orchard. First he clears it, then he fences it, breaks it up, plants it at considerable cost, and then he waits for a few years before seeing any returns. If he has made a bad start in selecting unsuitable land his prospects will be very dim and shadowy, and he may at last find all he has invested therein thrown away. There is no necessity for drawing upon the imagination for facts of this kind, for, unfortunately, they meet the eye at every turn. Gardens are started without judgment in this matter and without skill, and either through improper soil or indifferent treatment become failures and remain before the eyes of the would-be orchardists to scare them from making the attempt. The matter of soil selection, therefore, is of no little importance, and deserves the best thought and attention. Although the colony is young it is nevertheless old enough to have swallowed up a great amount of time, labour, and money in making failures of this kind and thus dearly buying experience. But with proper soil and a favourable climate the possibilities of fruit-growing in this colony are great, and this may be stated with none the less confidence, notwithstanding all the scarecrows in the shape of failures on every hand. Fortunately for my argument it is possible to find an occasional one successful in fruit-growing although surrounded by failures; and it may be safely asserted that what one man succeeds in doing is quite sufficient to prove the thing possible, let ever so many make failures besides. Majorities may be allowed to carry the sway in many things, but a minority in this is overwhelming proof the thing can be done. What makes the difference between the many failures and the one success is the very thing that needs to be worried out—so to speak—for until it is made plain the industry must languish for want of energetic men to take it up. The causes of failures in the abstract are legion; but upon careful examination they will resolve themselves into a few plain items, which may be expressed in such words as carelessness, slovenliness, idleness, and ignorance. The policy which aims at taking all that is possible from the soil with as little expenditure of labour and so forth upon it as possible, is a bad and ruinous one. It gives satisfaction nowhere, and is utterly at variance with modern ideas of progression and civilisation, for it is part and parcel of barbarism. In this age of rapid travelling and electric modes of thought and expression we aim at obtaining rapid results in everything, and advanced ideas in the art of cultivation agree with this. We study science and art to obtain the knowledge and mastery of those processes by which such results may be achieved, and having found them the course is open to apply them and reap the results. Thorough cultivation is the application of these principles, and it is the only cultivation at the present time giving good and satisfactory results.

Much of the success for which the fruit-grower labours is, as already stated, dependent upon the fitness of the soil for his trees.

There are no fruits grown but what gather most of their sustenance from the soil, and consequently the food they need must be in the soil for them to thrive and do well, and if it is not there naturally, artifice is called for to supply the want, or the attempt will prove a failure more or less complete. But all fruits, like other plants, do not require the same food, and as a necessary inference no one soil can be expected to produce all kinds of fruit equally well. Both climate and soil have to be taken into account before making a start, or, at least, before venturing farther than an experiment. In the absence of reliable information on this or any kindred subject it is often advisable to ask a question from Nature, by trying an experiment carefully and waiting and watching patiently for an answer. Individual soils will often call for some such method, for it is impossible to lay down any hard-and-fast rules whereby to judge the quality and productiveness of soils. There are general principles, however, which underlie this matter, which if duly apprehended at the outset and acted upon throughout seldom fail to give satisfaction. The soil which may be looked upon as necessary for the apple, pear, plum, cherry, fig, gooseberry, currant, and raspberry, is a rich deep alluvial soil with a well-drained subsoil, either naturally or artificially so. Many other fruit, such as the guava, jack-fruit, quince, medlar, bread-fruit, mulberry, banana, and pine-apple, and also the citron family, will do well in a similar soil; still they are, as a rule, better served with an underlying substrata of rock, or even a free admixture of it in the worked portion of the soil itself. The trees first mentioned draw heavily from the soil, and hence the fitness of extra fertility to enable the land to bear the strain. The grape, olive, orange, lemon, and the whole of this large and important family, appear to be much more thrifty and healthful where rock of some kind abounds, and if 1 were selecting a piece of land for a general orchard it would be a soil at least moderately fertile with a free admixture of broken rock—either limestone, basalt, granite, or even quartz, slate, and sandstone. This opinion is based upon observation and experience, for in all my travels I never saw as good results from trees grown in deep alluvial soils as I have witnessed from orchards where the soil and subsoil consisted largely of rock. These observations are also in perfect harmony with the teachings of science, for agricultural chemists declare that much of the fertility of the soil is owing to the decomposition of the rocks which form its base, and many of these mineral fertilisers are special manures for a number of our most valuable fruits. At the same time, it is not for me to say in so many words wherein these fertilising elements consist, for that is within the province of the analytical chemist alone. Another very vexed question bearingly closely upon the successful cultivation of the orange and related fruits, it appears to me, the agricultural chemist alone can answer satisfactorily. The orange may often be seen in one plot of ground thrifty and fruitful, and in land immediately adjoining, tilled the same and by the same workman, they are anything but a success. A case of this kind has passed under my notice, the soil in both plots being equally fertile but widely different. In both cases the drainage was the same—good—the subsoil being open and porous, both being on steep hillsides with the deep basin of a creek and permanent water between them. A careful analysis would probably disclose the important secret, and the discovery, if made, would be likely to remove one of the main obstacles to successful orange-growing out of the way. Several other facts which have come under my notice and which have a practical bearing upon this branch of my subject it may be as well to cite here. Some of the finest orange trees in Queensland—or, as is said by some, in all Australia—are to be found in the garden of a squatter in the Central districts. The surface soil is a black friable loam, and then comes rock, broken and open enough for the roots to penetrate freely. This is well drained naturally, and could not be improved upon by art in this particular. This land when trenched looked like a newly-formed and well-metalled road. In the Central districts, again—not far from the coast, but in a widely different soil—are other orange trees equally vigorous and fruitful. The soil here is a white calcareous gravelly stuff full of flinty stones, anything but easy to work, and the opposite of tempting for the cultivator to take in hand, and yet it produces good fruit, and plenty of it, when rich alluvial lands not far away will not. It is no easy matter often for even an experienced eye to decide upon the merits of a piece of land for fruit-growing, for the difference between two pieces is often more real than apparent. The best guide is the nature of the rocks most abundant in the locality, and which may be taken as forming the base of the soil, and the nature and quantity of the herbage indigenous thereto. Fertility in the soil is invariably indicated by thick and luxuriant grasses where the country is open, or by masses of thick scrub of the soft-wooded varieties when scrub land is called in question. A thick scrub or undergrowth of eucalypti or acacias is no indication of fertility, for they often are found on barren rocky hillsides where the grass never can be made to grow luxuriantly. It has been said, with a good show of reason, that land capable of producing quantities of heavy timber cannot be far out for fruit-producing also. This might mislead unless the varieties of timber were also taken into the account. Such trees as the flooded-gum, blue-gum, and mahogany thrive in ill-drained land, as also the swamp-oak and many others; and, on the other hand, the scented-gum, spotted-gum, stringy-bark, messmate, and some varieties of the box, attain to great size in soil where little grass will grow, or what is generally termed "barren stony ridges"; so that the notion that fruit trees may be expected to thrive wherever heavy timber has been must be taken *cum grano salis*. At the same time, many of these heavily timbered and almost grassless ridges could be converted into profitable vineyards or oliveyards, and put to good use for sericultural purposes by planting them with mulberries, or in the tropical north they may eventually prove suitable for the cinchona, ceara-rubber, and many of the valuable spices, and also for coffee. As a rule, the rich scrub lands of the colony are admirably adapted for fruit, and the best of these lands invariably have an underlying substratum of rock of an open nature. Land of a basaltic or volcanic origin, or land overlying a limestone or a granite formation, if well drained, is well calculated to carry fruit of any description; and some of the most valuable fruits—notably, the grape—are known to do well where quartz, feldspar, porphyry, or other hard and flinty rocks preponderate. If anything is to be gathered from these remarks of a general nature with reference to the soil suitable for fruit, it is that land is most reliable for the purpose where plenty of broken rock underlies a good surface soil, which is preferable in all cases to even deep rich alluvial soil when free from rock. There are exceptions to the rule which are not calculated to interfere materially with it, and a careful analysis would possibly show a closer resemblance between them than is to the eye apparent.

METHOD OF CULTIVATION.

With reference to cultivation, there are well-proved methods adapted to all kinds of fruit alike, and first in order after the choice of soil is its preparation for the reception of the young trees. What progress a newly-planted tree shall make is very much under the control of the planter. Vigorous growth can alone be secured by thorough preparation of the soil and liberal treatment in every particular. Those who plant trees for fruit or ornamentation are naturally anxious to see them thrive and grow vigorously, and, in the majority of cases, the desired result may be attained by the expenditure of a certain amount and quality of labour in thoroughly breaking and aërating the soil, and in the judicious application of good fertilisers. With trees of any value, or expected to become such, half measures in preparing land for their reception are, to say the least of it, very unwise. It is for results they are planted, and when they are stinted and starved to begin with how can the desired results be forthcoming? In general terms, then, thoroughness in cultivation is advisable to give young trees a chance, and what that thoroughness should consist in will now be particularised. In a Queensland climate, where prolonged droughts are so frequently experienced, there is no operation more absolutely necessary to the health and vigour of any tree than what is generally designated "trenching." When properly done it is almost a substitute for irrigation, possessing, however, one very great advantage over the latter, inasmuch as it can be generally applied to hills and in every situation where the artificial application of water is almost out of the question. But while speaking of trenching in the abstract it is necessary to state as clearly as possible in what the operation consists. In few words, it consists in breaking up and aërating the soil to the depth required—from 18 inches to 3 or even 4 feet; the latter depth, however, is seldom attempted, and only in very exceptional circumstances can it be recommended. The method of performing this operation, so long as it is done systematically, is a matter of perfect indifference, so long as it is done to one uniform depth throughout. This item needs to be especially enforced, however, for in retentive or strong soils irregularity in the level at the bottom of the trenching allows water to stagnate, often causing disease and death, to the astonishment or dismay of the proprietor of the orchard. Trench the land for your trees by all means, but be sure that the bottom is either porous, so that the water will soak away quickly, or make the bottom so that water cannot lodge there, by laying drains below the level of the bottom of the trenched land at intervals of every 5 or 6 yards, or between every row of trees.

Experience teaches unmistakeably that trenching should always be done with judgment rather than by any set rule. Any good pick and shovel man can do the work, but, before doing it, most people would act wisely by consulting some expert capable of giving certain and reliable ideas how that particular piece of land should be dealt with. The old practice of reversing the relative positions of soil and subsoil is fast becoming obsolete, and what is now sometimes called "double-digging" has in a general way taken its place. The modern method is certainly more in accordance with Nature, for her efforts are constantly to make and keep the best soil on the surface, and man errs most the more he departs from her sure guidance. Double-digging, as it is called, is quite as effective as the old method, and can be safely adopted where the other would do more harm than good. To "double-dig" first strip a trench of any desired length—say 2 feet wide by 12 feet long—of the surface spit, and wheel the removed soil to the immediate vicinity of the spot where you propose to finish the work. This done, break up the second spit without removing it, and, if it is heavy or strong, 2 or 3 inches of any rough hard material laid upon it before digging it and turning it under will help it wonderfully. This spit broken up, anything in the shape of vegetable matter may be spread upon it decomposed or otherwise. To finish the first trench proceed to take the top spit from a second one of the same size exactly, and lay it upon the first, breaking it up thoroughly meanwhile. Between the two layers a deposit may be made of rags, old boots, bones, maize-stalks, megass, dry grass, wood rubbish, seaweed—in fact, refuse of any description, for it can be put well out of sight and where it can at the same time be very useful. Proceed with the entire plot according to these directions, and if the land is not afterwards overcrowded with plants good results may be confidently looked for.

The common practice of preparing a small round hole 2 feet deep or more for the reception of the tree, and filling it in with good compost, cannot be recommended in any case for the reception of valuable trees; it is more like the work of the grave-digger doing the last service for man than the work of an intelligent cultivator. Even on sloping hillsides, in most places these holes are simply receptacles for stagnant water, which are productive of disease and death, instead of health, beauty, and fruitfulness, which are looked for. Where time is an object and double-digging cannot be done in season throughout, let a continuous strip be taken, 5 or 6 feet in width, and properly worked; the remainder to be done as opportunities offer. It may, however, be stated that this course is not advisable where first-class results are urgently called for. Anyone going to the expense of procuring valuable trees, either for ornamentation or fruit, should decide, also, as for an indispensable portion of the undertaking, to do all that lies in his power which the circumstances of the case demand to secure a success as far as possible, and so expedite their progress and bring them as early as possible to maturity. Occasionally it is reported that trenching land answers no good purpose; and very probably it is quite correct, simply because the soil is ill-drained and settles back again in a short time into as hard and impervious a state as before. In such cases trenching is worse than useless; it is positively injurious, for it takes in water which cannot escape and which is destructive to the porosity and fertility of the soil and of course the reverse of beneficial to the tree. In connection with this subject, therefore, that of draining land must come under attention also. The question is put at times, What benefit can follow from trenching sand or any light and porous soil? The question is practical and natural enough, but the only answer experience gives is that trenching even loose sand makes an immense difference in the productiveness of the soil. That is the fact; the wherefore of it is another thing. There is a natural and a sufficient reason for it undoubtedly if it could be discovered.

DRAINING LAND.

If any one operation is of more importance than another in the proper treatment and cultivation of fruit trees it is that of draining. In wet subsoils draining to carry away superfluous moisture, to a certain extent aërates the subsoil in consequence, and as this is the chief object of trenching it is easy to see how an orchard may be immensely benefited, and, in fact, positively enriched, by systematic drainage. Heretofore in this treatise wet land has been denounced as unsuited for fruit-growing; but if no other is available the inevitable must be accepted and made the best of. In that case, choose between thorough drainage or a miserable failure. Only in soils naturally so porous that the upper 4 feet will not hold water is draining uncalled for, and, as such are not invariably met with, draining may be calculated upon as part of the inevitable work to be done by gardeners and farmers. Bear in mind, also, that this applies with equal force to flat and ridgy land: an impervious subsoil must be drained to fit it for the reception of any valuable and permanent crop.

Unless the natural fall of the surface is slight it is not advisable to make the drains take the direction of the greatest fall; but rather take them in a sidling course, giving a good but not a great fall, to empty themselves at last into an open ditch or drain conveniently situated to receive the water from any number of branch ones on either side if required. Nor is it best to make branch drains at right angles to the main one, but more after the pattern set by Dame Nature in the matter of rivers and tributary creeks, or much as the network of a leaf is arranged in its midrib and veins leading thereto.

The aim should be to have the land drained and aërated everywhere 4 feet deep, and, whatever the labour and outlay thereby entailed, it has, in all instances where tried, proved to be most remunerative, its beneficial effects being shown from the outset and increasingly so as years rolled on. Any land with a sufficient tenacity of subsoil to hold water for twenty-four hours after rain requires draining, and water standing about the roots of plants works mischief much more certainly, and more frequently proves fatal, in a hot climate than in a cold one. All over the world it is found that vegetation will endure inundating or submerging in cold weather better than in hot, and taking peach trees as an apt illustration they frequently die suddenly in wet lands in Queensland during the wet and hot season. Every peach tree in a garden has been known to succumb under such circumstances, while in drained lands elsewhere and close by not one has suffered. Draining is therefore one of the great wants in Queensland, to allow vegetation of any description, more especially when of a permanent character like trees, to have anything like a chance.

Taking that as proved, the way to set about the work to best advantage may next be stated. As a rule, the best and cheapest materials for laying drains with are drain tiles; and everywhere near our large centres of population they are manufactured at a reasonable rate. In Brisbane the price per 1,000 is £5, and they could hardly be made cheaper. Proceeding on the directions given above, make your openings, if for tiles, as narrow as possible towards the bottom—if only wide enough to allow of laying the tile so much the better. Fit the tiles as closely as possible, and make no provision for allowing the water access into them, but around every joint work some well-tempered clay to make the joints close and thus keep loose earth from entering. In laying permanent drains with tiles, in England, it is the practice to ram clay close around the pipes, and this does not interfere in the least with the water working its way in. In heavy clay lands 18 feet apart is a good distance to lay the cross drains, and a 2-inch tile is found sufficient to carry all the water for a quarter of a mile at a stretch with only a slight fall.

In making orchards where stone is plentiful and easy to obtain, a good serviceable drain can be made to answer every purpose from them. Of course, to make a lasting drain with stones time must be taken to build them in at the bottom, so as to leave a clear run for the water without danger of choking. A very good plan is to arrange a row of stones of equal height on either side of a 1-foot drain, leaving from 3 to 5 inches clear in the centre, and box it in with flat stones at the top; for 1 foot above this fill in with loose stones—the smallest on the top—and cover with grass. Next tread a few inches of soft or tempered clay over the grass and fill in. Another method is to cut saplings to lay on either side at the bottom of the drain and cover them with hardwood slabs. It may be practicable to drain with stones or timber where tiles are altogether out of the question, and in such cases it will be found that good and effective drains can be made, if only proper care is taken, with the materials mentioned. One other method should also be mentioned, for it would possibly prove equal to draining with tiles if well done. Make a 6-inch wide drain at bottom, and fill in with good burning wood, such as brigalow, as closely as can be packed. Ram 6 inches or more of good clay over it, but previously cover the wood with a good layer of dried grass or leaves to keep the clay from driving through it. Let all the wood, &c., be well dried and ready to burn. When one length is finished kindle the wood at the lowest end of the drain to burn the wood out; this, in burning, will burn the clay sides, top and bottom, and leave a clear opening almost equal to a continuous drain tile. As a matter of course the success of this operation depends upon a sufficient draught being left to allow the wood to consume. If turned into charcoal it is an imperishable material, and will necessarily keep the ground open and allow free access to the water. Drains made according to the last method must be made while the land is dry to get them at their best.

Much in the matter of detail in connection with this important work may safely be left to any man with an average amount of common sense and ingenuity. One thing it will be necessary to enforce, viz., make all drains as far as possible from the rows of trees, because tree roots often find their way into them in masses and choke them. They are best at intermediate spaces between the rows. However the work is done let it be done thoroughly and done well, for it cannot be neglected without loss, whatever it may cost to do it. Many are prevented from draining because they are of opinion that it will rob growing crops of the moisture they need to keep them right. This is a very erroneous opinion, and often proves to be a serious or fatal mistake. Well-drained land is not the first to part with moisture in a time of drought. The reverse of this is true, for land which soddens or settles down close loses its moisture quickest, and the reason is it has not sufficient porosity to contain or hold water. Again, porosity is a bad conductor of heat. Honeycombed rock may lie exposed to the rays of the sun all day and the heat will hardly penetrate it; whereas if the rock is solid it will travel through it as through a solid bar of iron. Porosity of soil, then, prevents heat penetrating it (and cold likewise) and consequently reduces evaporation to a minimum. The special advantage claimed for a coating of mulch is based on this same principle and is known everywhere to work as stated. It is undoubtedly correct, then, that drained soil is necessarily more porous than undrained, and in the very nature of things must hold and retain moisture longer. All known facts also support this; and therefore all cultivators can be urged with the utmost confidence to commence and follow up this very important work with promptness and vigour.

PLANTING THE TREES.

With the foregoing preparations completed the next thing is "when" and "how" they shall be planted. As a preliminary it may here be stated that all virgin soil should enjoy a bare fallow for a few months before trees are put into it—that is, it should be trenched and in every way prepared for the reception of the trees so long before they are put out. Land is never ready for trees without this, nor will they be likely to make a good start otherwise. An apology for this consists in preparing a sufficiency of good rotten turf as a compost to plant each tree in, and if it is well done it is nearly an equivalent for the other.

When trees should be planted depends upon the locality, and whether they are tropical varieties or not. As a general rule, tropical fruit trees take most kindly to the removal in Queensland, more especially in the southern and cooler portions of it, when put out at the commencement of the growing season, and after all danger of cold from cutting westerly winds or frosts are past. This in Queensland is from September to, say, February. Other fruits, as a rule, are better planted as early as possible in the winter—the latter end of May is not too early—for one reason there is a better chance of sufficient moisture in the soil then than later on. But if the rainfall continues through the winter months, any time before the sap commences to rise will do, which may be set down as nearly as possible to the end of July. At the same time, it cannot be too emphatically stated that late planting is hazardous and not at all to be recommended, and only those who know exactly what they are about should think of doing it. Bananas and pine-apples can be planted with impunity during hot and wet weather. Cold is an enemy to both, and in cold or frosty weather they are more likely to die than live if in any way meddled with, except to mulch or otherwise protect them.

Tree-planting should be proceeded with as follows:—As far as possible plant all trees together which are either of one family or of the same habit of growth; for then the distances between them can be regulated more satisfactorily. All fruit trees do not require the same amount of room to develop in, which should be taken into account before starting so that the land may be laid out accordingly. The trees requiring the greatest amount of space are as nearly as possible the following:—The orange, lemon, shaddock, citron, some of the smooth-fruited custard-apples, mango, vee fruit, rose-apple, wampee, loquat, tamarind, apricot, mulberry, persimmon, jack-fruit, alligator pear, yellow guava, and the apple and pear. For these a space of 30 feet square is none too much unless the land is very poor, when they may be planted 5 or may be 10 feet closer, for they cannot grow so large to need the space. Cramping fruit trees is not the way to get the heaviest crops or the finest fruit; nor will a crowded orchard yield such good and regular crops as one judiciously planted in this particular. Many other fruits, such as the lime, cumquat, litchee, white, purple, and gooseberry guavas, some of the custard-apples (*anona squamosa* in particular), the peach, nectarine, almond, fig, longan, quince, Livingstone's mangosteen, the Cochin gorke, flacourtia, and others besides, will do with 20 feet square in rich land and from 15 to 18 feet in poorer. In rich deep soils everything planted requires more room, whether it be fruit trees, ornamental trees and shrubs, or smaller plants; for as they will naturally grow larger they want space to allow air and light to pass freely all through and among them. This matter of giving plants proper room is an essential not to be disregarded without loss, and more especially does this rule hold good with trees whose crop, and therefore entire value, is in the fruit they bear.

The next thing in planting is to procure a sufficient quantity of stakes about 1¼ or 1½ inches in diameter and 4 feet 6 inches long. Then take a garden reel and a long and stout line and drive the first stake in at half the distance from the fence each way that the trees are to be planted from each other. If, for instance, they are to be 30 feet apart put the stake in 15 feet from either fence. Proceed to the other end of the row and do the same, and then stretch the line between these two points and at every 30 feet drive in one of the stakes, putting them down 15 or 18 inches. Proceed in this way with the whole of the land to be planted, giving distance according to the directions already furnished. If the season is right for planting and the trees all ready, proceed at once with the work. Examine each tree as you plant it to see that it has no injured or bruised roots. If it has, take your pruning knife and make clean cuts in removing them; also trim the ends of all the strong root stumps back to where the bark and wood unite perfectly and are sound. Then examine the top and use the knife to cut it back with an eye to symmetry until the roots and tops are as nearly as possible in just proportions to each other, having no more top than roots to find food for them. This is an item of great importance and cannot be attended to too scrupulously, as it frequently makes all the difference there is between life and death to the trees. Next remove the soil all round the stake to a sufficient width and depth to allow of the roots being carefully spread out on every side, and so that the soil when filled in again will cover the top root with no more than an inch or so of soil. Then put in your tree close up to the stake and with the hand carefully spread the roots equally on all sides; then fill in with well pulverised soil, very gently shaking the tree meanwhile to get the fine earth down among the roots, and when the hole is nearly filled in press the earth to the roots with the foot—not too firmly if wet, but moderately firm if dry; then use water freely if dry, but if the land is wet use it only to wash the soil down among the roots. You may next fill in the remainder of the soil and level the surface, and as soon as possible after put all around the tree a good coating of mulch. Mulching is the very best safeguard against drought in tree-planting that can be used and should never be neglected. As a rule, trees are understood to be the better for tying to the stakes at the time of planting, but if the tops have been well headed back and little is left for the wind to lay hold of it may be dispensed with; in the majority of cases, however, the safest plan is to stake and tie securely. It is better to use no ties at all than poor ones; for staked trees if the ligatures break are easier injured and broken than though it had not been done; therefore stake and tie securely or leave it undone altogether. Proceed in this way carefully with every tree and do not forget the mulching, and then you will find that failures will be very few and far between, if there are any. Lest any of my readers should be at a loss about mulching, it is well to state that it consists in simply spreading long grass, spent bark from the tannery, partially decomposed manure, or any open porous material, upon the surface of the ground to prevent the sun's rays penetrating to bake the surface or exhaust the moisture by evaporation. Very little water serves to establish a tree and to get it to start when mulching is properly attended to, while on the other hand large quantities of water are, comparatively speaking, valueless without it.

But there are other fruits which must not be overlooked which do not come under the above category, and these are bananas and pine-apples. The land should be prepared for them the same as for other fruits, but put them in by themselves. To do well they require deep, rich, and well-worked land, and then in a suitable climate they will do wonders. Where the land is rich and deep, bananas of all kinds should have not less than 15 square feet to each plant, and even 20 feet in some instances is none too much. Whatever distance is right mark out the land with line and stakes as for other trees, and plant suckers not more than one-third grown. Firm them well with the foot and cut back all the leaves to give the wind as little as possible to lay hold of until they are established and start into growth; but you need not stake bananas. The Queen pine-apples are best planted in rows 8 feet apart and 3 feet from plant to plant; the smooth-leaved and larger ones require fully 2 feet more—that is, 10 feet—between the rows. This will leave good room for getting about among them to gather the crop and cultivate. Suckers about half grown make the best plants, and if the variety is a scarce and valuable one the tops of the fruit make excellent plants, only they take longer time to mature. And now, supposing all these instructions to have been attended to, the land well trenched, drained, carefully planted with good varieties of fruit adapted to the climate, and the trees well cared for in every respect, signs will not long be wanting that they are obeying the calls of Nature and starting into new growth.

Now for the after cultivation. Having done so much well it will not do to stop there; but you must follow on as you have begun. In this climate, where droughts are frequent, and, if anything, to be reckoned upon, do not try to raise anything but fruit in land allotted to it or "between two stools you will fall to the ground." Allowance may be made for the youth of the trees, seeing that for a while the roots cannot occupy the land, but even this is only true to a very small extent. Tree roots fill and occupy the land much more quickly and thoroughly than most people imagine. In a well-worked orchard where fruit trees are doing anything like well very little unoccupied land will be found in two or three years time, for the roots will pierce and penetrate it everywhere. Every other crop taken from the land, even while the trees are small and young, checks the advancement of the trees; and the most experienced orchardists question very much the wisdom of the policy which attempts taking anything else from the land after once the trees are planted. However, as so much labour and outlay has to be expended upon the land to get it in readiness for the trees, it is only natural to try and obtain an immediate return for this if possible ; and as it may be done with little risk so long as nothing is planted within several feet of the stem of the tree all round, it is the rule to give it a measure of countenance; at the same time, it is not correct. One thing must be here emphatically stated, and that is: the climate of Queensland will not allow of growing grass in an orchard, for the simple reason that the rainfall is altogether inadequate to support the two crops. In the moist climates of Great Britain and New Zealand, and some few favoured localities where irrigation is practicable, it may be otherwise, but to take pattern by these with such wide climatic differences is neither more nor less than a fatal mistake. Of the truth of this statement there are unfortunately very many clear proofs. The cleaner the land is kept the greater will be its productiveness, and that in all seasons, whether droughty or otherwise. This also applies with equal force to bananas and pine-apples. Let these valuable plants have all the land to themselves and they will mature much more rapidly and bear heavily, and at the same time the finest and best of fruit; while, if they are allowed to become over-run with grass and weeds, as is very frequently the case, they must be starved, and if you look to them for a living they will starve you. To get bananas to do their best in every respect they should systematically be prevented from multiplying their suckers indefinitely. It is out of the question to think a small patch of land can support a multitude of suckers at one stool, and bunches of fruit at the same time. Each stool should be allowed to show no more than two stems at once—the most forward with its bunch of fruit and the next coming on to succeed it. This is not theory; it is a well-tried and most successful method of treating the banana. An acre of bananas so treated will certainly produce more than two acres left to run into masses, and it will do it for a great number of years without exhausting the soil so rapidly. Bananas are known to produce the first bunch of ripe fruit from the planted sucker in very little over twelve months, and will keep up a succession in the shape of a large bunch within every six months after; whereas where bananas are left to "go-as-they-please" it is no uncommon thing to see small stems more than two years old which have never borne, and when the fruit does struggle into sight it is only a mere apology for a bunch of poor and miserable fruit. With reference to the thinning, another caution is necessary. To do it to any purpose a sharp spade must be used to cut each sucker clean away, with its butts and roots ; cutting them off level with the ground does no good. Of course this should be done as carefully as possible, so as not to cut the feeding roots of the remaining stems any more than is unavoidable ; but the plant left will suffer less if some of its roots are cut, so long as these robbers are taken away from them. Pine-apples cannot be so well thinned. The better plan is to cultivate them well and keep them at it until they become small and weedy, and then make a new plantation in fresh ground, trying some other crop on the land for a while to thereby restore it. Both bananas and pine-apples pay best when treated liberally, and yield all the heavier crop if manured plentifully. The banana is a particularly gross feeder and quickly exhausts the land.

PRUNING FOR FRUIT.

Much of what has been already written has to do with the after culture of the orchard; but while treating upon the tillage of the soil the important operation of pruning must not be overlooked. No operation in the wide range of orchard work is of more importance than pruning, and, as everyone knows, none is more systematically neglected. To a certain extent this neglect is caused by the idea that it can only be done serviceably by a professional. That may or may not be true; unfortunately, professionals—not a few—are as unreliable with the knife as many amateurs, and amateurs gifted with a fair share of common sense and quick powers of observation will do better work with pruning tools than a so-called professional.

Pruning needs to be regularly attended to or left undone altogether—that is to say, it should be done every season as it comes round. Although an artificial operation, it is, if properly attended to, in perfect harmony with Nature. Once doing it certainly makes its continuance the more compulsory, as is said to be the case with bleeding, now almost obsolete in the practice of medicine; but it never can be well done without, and as an adjunct to high-class cultivation may be regarded as indispensable. It finds its place in gardening operations as being somewhat anticipatory of Nature's method of getting rid of worn-out wood; and, where appearances are also studied, is unquestionably much better. For instance, leave a peach-tree to itself, uncared for and unpruned; what would be the result? It would grow and bear heavily for a year or two when sufficiently matured, and would then rapidly become misshapen, barren, and useless; while, with proper attention with the knife, as great a weight of fruit will have been ripened by it in the time and the tree maintained in luxuriance and fruitfulness. This being so, pruning cannot be at variance with Nature, but must, on the contrary, be helpful to it. And what is here said of the peach applies with equal force to any other fruit-bearing tree. Let the advocates of non-pruning illustrate their case with as good a show of reason as the advocate of pruning does, and then men of common sense will listen and obey; but it cannot be. The object of pruning is to preserve the tree or plant in as healthful and vigorous a condition as possible and for a prolonged period; and if it cannot be shown that pruning, judiciously and seasonably done, is beneficial, let it be summairly abandoned.

The tools requisite for a large amount of pruning are a good pruning saw, a pruning knife, and one or two sizes of French or English pruning shears. Added to them must also be a pair of stout leathern gloves—fear-noughts—with which the thorny citrus family may be fearlessly approached. Of course, the owner of a small garden containing but a few trees may do all the work he requires with a good pruning knife, an ordinary saw, and a handy little pair of pruning shears. Another useful pruning tool has been invented and patented in America recently—a pruning chisel—said to be very effective in lopping off large branches when out of reach, and as it makes a clean cut it is likely to prove a decided acquisition. Saws and scissors, it is necessary to state, are both objectionable tools, as they make an ugly cut, which stands in the way of rapid healing. In pruning it is understood that the cut should be a clean one—that is, perfectly smooth on the surface—with the bark uninjured and intact to the margin of the cut. Neither a saw nor a pair of shears can make such a cut, and therefore with all particular work it is customary to follow both these tools with a very keen strong knife, and trim the ragged and uneven cuts to a smooth surface. Nor is this practice uncalled for; it is in unison with Nature's requirements, and allows of healing, and that rapidly, where otherwise it would never be possible.

Pruning for fruit is the idea. Pruning for leaves or wood is all very well for the sericulturist or in a tea plantation, but in an orchard it would be altogether out of place. All trees cannot be pruned after one model, but every tree must be dealt with after its nature or according to its habit of bearing. This remark applies also to a limited extent even to individual trees of one kind, because all will not grow and bear exactly alike, and pruning should always be done according to the individual requirements of each particular tree. To know how to prune any given tree, its habit of bearing—whether on the young shoots, or on short spurs projecting from the old wood—has to be taken into account, and the work done accordingly. The peach, almond, mulberry, nectarine, and apricot are much alike in this respect, and bear, principally at least, on the ripened wood of the previous year's growth. When these drop their leaves and are ready for the knife the flower buds are mostly showing, so that a mere tyro in pruning can scarcely make a mistake if he properly uses his eyes. These require cleaning out in the centre of all shoots that are weak and straggling, and which cross other branches and chafe, continuing until the centre is moderately open, but in Queensland not open enough to allow the noontide rays of a tropical sun to concentrate its fervour upon the leafless and unshaded wood. Next proceed to shorten back all the strongest leading shoots which are set well for bloom, and make the ends as snug and trim as can be done judiciously. Then finally cut clean out any misplaced or spent branches, leaving no heel to die and form a spur of unsightly wood. When done the tree should be everywhere even, well balanced, and capable of feeling the influence of air and light everywhere through it, without the constant rays of the sun beaming anywhere. Then there are the apple, pear, plum, and cherry, all which bear their fruit on short spurs which project an inch or two from the wood of the matured branches. In pruning for fruit these spurs must be looked for, and only when the branches carrying them are misplaced or spent should they be separated from the tree. Whenever branches cross each other and chafe one of them is misplaced and should be cut clean out to save the other. As a rule, weak shoots, crowded, misplaced, or exhausted wood, and the long straggling points of the main shoots are what should be cut away. Always keep the general symmetry of the tree in view while pruning, and to know whether the knife should be used unsparingly or otherwise observe whether the tree is growing vigorously or not. Where the tree is vigorous and running away to wood prune little; where it is wanting in vigour either cut it until you can compel it to make fresh wood, or use some fertiliser to force it to grow, and even then prune heavily. A tree running into wood has generally more roots and feeding ground than top to absorb it, and *vice versâ* when wood is scantily formed. The correct pruning for a tree making too much wood is at the roots; they are too many for the top, and cutting the top makes matters worse. Root-pruning in such cases often throws a formerly barren tree into bearing. Then there are trees which bear from the extreme points of the shoots, such as the mango, wampee, litchee, and many others; shortening back is not the pruning for them. Unless points of branches are left somewhere on them to break into bloom the fruit crop will be a failure; but it does no follow that the longest leading branches should be left entire. Whenever the balance of the tree admits of it do so; but when leaving them entire causes a straggling tendency through weakness, shorten them back to some of the laterals, which leave entire, or cut some clean out if these are numerous or crowded. In other respects simply work by the rule already given of admitting a free circulation of air and light everywhere by a judicious thinning of the poorest, weakest, and most ill-placed wood. The orange and citrus family generally bear on the wood of the previous year's growth. The best general rule to observe in pruning these is to subject the whole tree to a careful thinning, cutting out always what can best be spared and having an eye to the balance of the tree and its general symmetry. This simple rule is good for a much wider application; in fact, the amateur may act upon it in a general way, not only with impunity, but also beneficially.

Then there is vine-pruning. This is a speciality and deserves separate treatment, but the following must suffice in this connection:—Like the peach, it bears its crops upon the wood of the previous season, and just enough of this must be left to do its work and no more. In pruning the vine use every endeavour to keep old gnarled and twisted lumps and knots from accumulating at the bases of the branches, and to do this allow new wood to make occasionally below, so that all above may from time to time be removed. In other respects shorten all the bearing wood to within two or three eyes of the point of starting, and cut clean out all weak and worthless wood. A good knife or a handy pair of *secateurs* will do the work very expeditiously, and when it is well done you can reckon on a paying crop of good fruit; but vines neglected in this respect are worthless.

Another kind of pruning called sometimes "spring pruning" and at others "finger-and-thumb pruning" is an equally important operation. This is done in the spring, when the sap is rising and shoots are breaking out all over the tree, many of which are not wanted. To allow these to grow merely to cut them off again in the winter is a waste of the energies of the tree. By rubbing them off while tender, and leaving only what are required, the sap of the tree is directed into useful channels and a saving in every way is effected. This is an exceedingly simple and effective operation, and no careful orchardist can afford to neglect it.

With reference to root-pruning, it is very easy to know when it will be likely to benefit the tree. For an illustration, suppose a tree is growing into a large spreading tree, and you look for fruit on it but find none. The vigour of the tree proves that it is not wanting manure, but it wants something. In that case, try pruning the roots. To do it, make a circular trench at an equal distance all round the tree, keeping at or near the outer spread of the branches. Clean out the trench to the full depth of the lowest roots, cutting every root back with a clean cut from a sharp knife to the inner side of the trench, and then fill back the soil again; it is usual, before filling-in the soil, to employ some good stimulant or fertiliser. Another good plan to throw a woody vigorous tree into bearing is to tie ligatures round the stems of the main branches, which will check the flow of sap and also the formation of wood, while fruit buds and spurs will form, and the tree often blossoms and bears heavily, and then the ligatures should be removed. There is yet another good method of throwing fruit trees shy of fruiting into good bearing, which is as follows:—Cut a few stakes, from 2 to 3 feet in length. Drive them firmly into the ground in a circle round the tree a little distance short of where the branches reach. Fasten a ring of No. 6 wire to the top of the stakes and then proceed carefully to bring down the branches, one by one, and secure them with some soft tying material as regularly as possible all round. This will have the effect of checking the flow of sap, thereby preventing excessive luxuriance in making wood, and fruit buds will form. In the warmer portions of Queensland the apple and pear are often brought into bearing by this treatment, and the same rule will apply equally well with many other fruits.

GRAPE CULTURE.

But the grape vine requires a little special consideration when treating of fruits suitable for Queensland. This fruit is a study in itself, and yet it is as easy to manage as any known fruit, and quite as profitable. All grapes, except the Scuppernong and its varieties, require much the same treatment, and as this once vaunted vine has received like condemnation from all who have given it a trial in this colony, it may well be passed with the contempt it merits in this treatise. Trenched land, in the first place, may be regarded as a *sine quâ non*. Fruit may be and is raised without it, but no one who has had an acquaintance with the difference between trenching and shallow working in the cultivation of this fruit would hesitate for one moment as to the proper course to pursue. One great reason why trenching is invaluable to the vine is that it bears mostly during the driest season of the year, and consequently ground worked only a few inches is quickly dry, and unless rain comes frequently the fruit perishes altogether or ripens miserably small and wanting in proper flavour. It is easy to see, therefore, that the advantages are decidedly in favour of trenching for vines. Draining is equally necessary, but that has been sufficiently considered already in a former part of this treatise. If a large area of land is to be planted, procure a sufficiency of good cuttings and insert them perpendicularly in the soil, one in a place where they are to remain, covering them to within an inch or so of the top eye or bud. If the planting is done late, insert two cuttings. The distance allowed between them must, in a measure, be regulated by variety and soil. Many of the American varieties, and notably the Isabella, require fully 8 feet square to each plant—that is 8 feet from plant to plant. Some of the more delicate European kinds will do with 5 feet or 6 feet. In rich deep soils it is necessary to allow the greater space for all. In the cooler districts, and where they are grown extensively for wine-making purposes, it is customary to tie each plant to a single stake. The trellis system, however, is very decidedly the best, whenever it is at all practicable, and in gardens no other way should be thought of. Good hardwood stakes driven in every 12 feet, having been previously charred where they are to go underground, and wires secured to them (either by staples or by boring the posts), to the height of 4 feet from the ground, and three wires stretched at equal distances, the lowest from 1 foot to 15 inches above the ground, the top one level with the top of the stakes, and the other midway between. No. 6 or No. 8 wire (galvanised) will do. This will make a cheap, neat, and durable trellis. As the vine is a potash plant, fresh wood ashes and bone dust are excellent fertilisers. The pruning of the vine has been already considered, but it may be well to add to the foregoing that vines trained on a trellis require to be left longer than when tied to stakes; not too long, or more fruit will show than the plant can mature and much or all of it will be lost.

Another important Queensland fruit is the annual hibiscus, commonly known as the rosella. It is easily raised from seed and the only treatment it needs is about the same as is given to cabbages, only it will thrive and do well in much poorer soil. In poor soil plant them 6 feet apart each way, and in rich soil 8 feet. This fruit, because of its agreeable acidity and wholesomeness, deserves to be grown extensively for making into preserves and drying, and would be a readily marketable commodity either way. Enterprise and spirit to carry on the industry properly would undoubtedly make it highly remunerative.

PICKING AND PACKING.

Picking and packing fruit for market are operations requiring to be done with care and intelligence. Due regard must first be paid to the distance the fruit has to be carried to market and the materials readily available for packing. As a rule, no fruit should be gathered until fully ripe, but when the grower has to look to a distant market for the sale of it the exigencies of the case demand that this rule be overlooked. Ripe fruit will not carry far without bruising and decomposing, an evil greater than marketing it before fully ripe. No method has yet been discovered, save that of jam-making and drying, by which it can be marketed in a sound and wholesome condition. The only thing to be done, then, is carefully to pick the fruit when its growth is matured and while it is still firm, only wanting the final ripening process. Apples, pears, plums, grapes, can all be gathered thus for sending long distances, if only they are carefully handled so as to prevent bruising. Grapes should be nearly ripe before they are picked. Mangoes, custard-apples, pine-apples, and bananas can also be picked under-ripe and sent considerable distances without being injured. Oranges, lemons, limes, shaddocks, and citrons are fruits that carry well if not allowed to get too ripe before being gathered, so also the fruit of *passiflora edulis* (the common passion-fruit); the granadillas, *passiflora quadrangularis* and *macrocarpa*, will not carry far without injury, being externally soft. Any fruit requiring to be kept should always be cut from the tree and not plucked. Guavas, figs, and all the berry fruits will not keep or carry in the fresh state, but require to be marketed close at hand and within a few hours of being gathered, unless dried or otherwise preserved. What some of the many new preservatives and antiseptics may do for the fruit-grower in the important matter of delaying its decomposition it is premature to say, but it appears highly probable that it will introduce a new era and cause a fresh departure altogether. Glacialine is fast coming into favour as a very useful antiseptic, and does nearly all that is claimed for it; so it will probably serve for preserving ripe fruit from decomposition.

Picking being a necessary preliminary to packing, and requiring equal care, the foregoing remarks were indispensable. The great thing in packing fruit is to see that they are put in snug and close and remain so. If they are packed carelessly and loosely, so that in shaking they move about, they cannot long continue sound. Apples, pears, oranges, lemons, shaddocks, and citrons are all sent on long sea voyages by simply packing them in moderately small cases to hold a bushel or less as above described, and without packing material of any description. Plums, cherries, and gooseberries are sent away in smaller cases still, but not such distances, and the same may be also said of peaches, nectarines, and apricots. Careful packers have successfully tried the covering of apples with fine tissue paper; Californian apples especially have been sent all over the world packed thus. Packing in dry sawdust is very good for many of the above fruits, but on account of the trouble to collect the material is likely to prove objectionable, especially while it can be so well done without. Grapes being a more thin-skinned and tender fruit need some such protection to carry long distances, and dry sawdust has proved an excellent material for shaking in among the fruit after being first packed snug and close. In packing fruit for market no reasonable time taken in keeping them in saleable condition is lost, for the condition of the fruit is everything to the salesman. In cool or refrigerating chambers, pine-apples packed carefully with sawdust, and bananas likewise, could be carried by mail steamers to Europe, and landed in good condition, for the experiment has been already successfully tried.

But the banana can be treated successfully in another way for sending long distances by simply gathering the fully ripe fruit and dipping the bunch into boiling water for two or three seconds, then remove the skins and pack them closely together in small boxes like those used for dates and raisins, or they may be wrapped singly in the wrappers stripped from maize cobs and packed in that way. As stated before, however, we are on the eve of a fresh departure in the matter of preserving, and therefore carrying fruits and other things over the world, and probably things now unthought of, will soon become matter of fact.

MARKETABLE VALUE.

As a matter of course, the market value of any commodity—fruit, or ought else—is regulated by the well-known laws of demand and supply, and is therefore at all times liable to fluctuations. Then again, there are qualities in fruit, such as superior varieties and well-grown samples also, which in the very nature of things command a better figure than poorer kinds or inferior samples. Making fair allowances for this, the price in the local or colonial markets for Queensland fruits will be found much as follows:—Oranges, 7s. to 14s. per case of 12 dozen; lemons, 12s. to 20s. per case of similar size; bananas, according to quality, from 4d. to 6d. per dozen; pine-apples (Queen's), from 1s. to 4s. per dozen; Cayenne or smooth-leaved pines, from 10s. to 25s. or more per dozen; cocoanuts, from 15s. to 20s. per hundred; mangoes, 2s. and 3s. per dozen; custard-apples, from 3s. to 4s. per dozen; limes and cumquats, 3d. or 4d. per lb.; grapes, from 2d. to 3d. per lb., and at times lower; granadillas, 3s. to 4s. per dozen; common passion-fruit, 3d. and 4d. per dozen; papaws, according to size, from 2s. to 3s. per dozen; jack-fruit, from 1s. 6d. to even 3s. or 4s. each. All these fruits are grown in Queensland, and most of them, up to the present time, have been marketed in the immediate neighbourhood or in the adjoining colonies. The fruits of the temperate zone, such as the apple, pear, plum, quince, &c., although grown in Queensland, do not mature in sufficient quantities to be considered under this heading, the other colonies suiting their production much better.

With reference to the value of Queensland fruits in the markets of Europe but little can be said, for up to the present no trial of any significance has been made, nor are any of her specialities in this respect quoted in the "prices current" issued from the old country markets. Pine-apples are highly appreciated everywhere, and at some seasons of the year sell in England as high as 1s. 6d. to 2s. per pound; grapes also at times fetch high prices, as much as 2s. 6d. per pound for good samples being freely paid; oranges and lemons are usually in good supply from the Madeira Islands, the Brazils, the West Indies and Florida, and prices are frequently below those quoted in the local markets; mangoes are almost unheard of in

European markets, although there is every reason to believe an effort to land them there in good condition would be substantially rewarded, for amongst the nobility the fruit is held in high esteem ; bananas are also well known and much relished in the old country, and would, if landed in good condition, at times realise a better price than they fetch here ; but they are occasionally in large supply ; quotations for the latter are seldom given. Tropical fruits, as a rule, are a very uncertain commodity anywhere in Europe, seldom seen, and of course but little known ; it cannot, therefore, be expected that prices can be given, seeing that to a great extent the market requires to be made for them, and to as great an extent also the taste for them acquired.

COFFEE.

Strictly speaking coffee is not what is usually considered a fruit, still, as it bids fair to become a product of Queensland ere long, it will not be out of place to briefly consider it in this connection.

There are two varieties of coffee—Arabica and Liberian ; the latter is more tropical and tender than the former, but it is also more prolific, and is found to resist the leaf disease now devastating the coffee plantations of Ceylon. Coffee of superior quality has been grown at Mackay, by Mr. Costello, of the Millicent Plantation, and the Liberian coffee is doing and bearing well on the Herbert River. With reference to what is known as "Mocha" coffee, it is simply the smallest berries of the Arabica which shell out in the oval form, and are found somewhat superior in flavour to the split berries which grow on the same tree.

Coffee requires raising in nursery beds and then to be transplanted. The spring of the year—say August or September—is the best season to sow the seed. The seed should be fresh berries as they come from the tree. To be able to manipulate them properly lay out beds from 3 feet to 3 feet 6 inches wide, making the surface up with some rich and light compost. In a bed 10 or 12 feet long plants enough may be raised for several acres at 8 feet apart each way. A strip of dead and decaying turf about 4 inches wide laid under each drill at the depth of 6 inches would facilitate matters in transplanting, filling up above the turf with rich compost. Sow the seed about an inch deep, firming it in gently with the foot, and watering it thoroughly. If the bed is kept moist the seeds will germinate in a fortnight or a little more, and in a month or six weeks be ready for transplanting.

The preparation required for the crop depends very much upon soil and situation. In rich porous scrub lands on hillsides a rough kind of terracing would serve the purpose, allowing a row of trees to each terrace. In low-lying rich lands, clear of couch and troublesome weeds, if naturally well drained, holes may be prepared with a little extra soil to give the young plants a strong start, and the remainder of the land kept clean with hoeing. If, however, couch is plentiful, and the land is hard and heavy, coffee will make very unsatisfactory headway unless thorough cultivation is employed. If labour can be had the better plan in all cases is to adopt thoroughness in cultivation, for with it there will be fewer failures and less frequent disappointments. Arabica will do 8 feet apart, but the Liberian, being stronger and more luxuriant, should have at least 10 feet. When ready for transplanting, and the weather being moist, peg out your land. Then lift your plants with all possible care to preserve the roots intact, and lay them in a basket, shading them therein from the influences of wind and sun. Having put in your plant near the stake, press the earth firmly around it, water it, and then with a few leafy boughs or Zamia leaves shade it. Proceed in the same way to the end. In dry or windy weather watch the newly-planted trees, and if any sign of dryness shows in the soil water them, for until they take and start to grow a little drought will settle them. When once established the shading should be removed, and then for two or three years, until they begin to bear, the land will need only such attention as keeping it thoroughly clear of weeds and the surface loose.

When the trees have grown to the height of 4 or $4\frac{1}{2}$ feet, the top should be removed, and any attempt made to run upwards should be prevented As a matter of course this will tend to throw the tree into wood below, and pruning will be necessary to check it. The wood of the coffee tree requires the influence of the sun and air to ripen it and make it fruitful just as other fruits do; and therefore, unless the branches are kept somewhat open, so that they can be seen through, the crop must be light. The shortening back of the top is followed on coffee plantations to make the work of gathering the crop suitable for women and children.

Ripe coffee is berry-like, deep crimson in colour, and oval in shape, and somewhat smaller than a cherry. The smaller berries contain only one oval bean; the larger ones split in two, and, as already stated, these are separated and sold so under the respective names of Mocha and Arabica. The ripe coffee-berry is very tempting to fruit-eating birds, a variety of the pied crow shrike being exceedingly partial to them.

COFFEE-TEA.

When pruning, utilise the leaves as follows:—Strip them from the stems while green and dry them on iron plates in a brisk heat until they show signs of brittleness, and then they may be used instead of tea and but few will despise them. In Java and other coffee countries the leaves are by many esteemed more than the berries, and, speaking from my own experience, I most decidedly say they are really excellent.

In concluding this brief chapter it may be worth while recording a very simple and efficient method employed in India for watering a coffee plantation. Porous water-bottles, capable of holding about a gallon of water, are sunk into the ground near the roots of the tree, and filled from time to time with water, which escapes by the pores slowly and waters the tree. A stone shuts up the mouth to keep small animals from entering. An area of somewhat larger size, similarly situated and filled with stones, would serve much the same purpose.

ORANGE CULTURE.

INTRODUCTORY.

The subject of orange cultivation is one of more than ordinary importance to Queensland occupiers of the soil, for the orange is a fruit as widely appreciated as any known to the pomologist, and it would appear to be pretty much at home in our Queensland soil and climate. This very thing is, however, at the present time decidedly a moot question with many who have, at least, made an attempt at orange culture. From some cause which they are utterly unable to define their efforts have not been seconded by Dame Nature as they had fondly anticipated, and failure more or less has been the result. At the commencement of any important industry every likely avenue of danger or probable cause of failure calls for the closest of watchfulness and attention, to guard, as far as possible, against its occurrence, and the orange has so far proved to be a very difficult subject to manage. Anyone who has had the opportunity of seeing the orange in the thousand and one places it has been, or is being tried in this colony, must have felt at times more or less puzzled or perplexed with what appeared. Without travelling far—often within the compass of a mile, or even much less—orange-trees will have shown remarkably healthy and fruitful, and others as conspicuously the reverse close by. At times very healthy, large, and fruitful specimens show themselves in what appears to be hungry and barren soil; again, the same may be seen in a rich deep alluvial deposit; and as fine specimens, in other cases, will be found in a friable black loam overlying a substrata of broken rock. Strong soils, sandy loams, black clayey and chocolate soils are to be seen producing as healthy and satisfactory specimens of this valuable fruit tree as could be desired; and, unfortunately, as frequently the reverse. The question naturally arises, "What can be the reason for such apparent differences?" Evidently some cause or causes are widely operative in nullifying human efforts at orange culture; and success is entirely dependent upon getting at the root of the matter, so that the axe of intelligent treatment may be persistently and successfully used against it. That the orange-tree can be grown successfully is already abundantly shown, but it as clearly appears difficult to command such success.

The difficulties surrounding this question are made all the more insurmountable, at least to the majority, by the many conflicting opinions held by men who have gathered their experiences under widely different circumstances. Men with a large and varied experience in matters horticultural are often free enough in confessing that the orange-tree is a perfect puzzle to them. The theories advanced by men who have enjoyed good opportunities of experimenting with the orange have, as frequently as not, exploded and proved worthless when applied elsewhere ; and hence the great puzzle it has become to the most experienced. And now, after admitting so much, it may well be asked, " What have you to offer better than others have already set before us?" On that point I will not hazard an opinion. My experience and observation has brought me face to face with all the difficulties of the subject, and therefore, as a practical man, if I cannot claim to see clearly through them to the end, I can very plainly see a large amount of data to go upon that will help greatly in guarding against many failures and go a long way to ensure a certain amount of success in such an important undertaking.

INTERVIEWING DAME NATURE.

One of the first things to take into consideration in a subject like this is, " What are the fair deductions to be drawn from the history of successful orange culture elsewhere?" When difficulties confront us in connection with any branch of science our wisest plan is at once to interview Dame Nature and endeavour to get her advice and assistance. There are natural laws which lie at the root of all successes, and to master these laws is the first and highest attainment, and next to that is the successful application of them. One of the first things which strike the inquiring and observant mind is that the orange-tree is quite semi-tropical. To extremes of heat or cold it appears to be alike sensitive. In Queensland the orange-tree is in its greatest vigour and healthfulness during spring and autumn, and where the winters are mild and free from frost that vigour is sustained quite through the winter. Great sun-heat tends as much to check its growth and induce disease as frost, and if anything it is even more injurious. Where the temperature in the shade seldom exceeds 80 degrees Fah. in summer and as rarely sinks below 40 degrees in winter, the orange-tree wonderfully luxuriates. The temperature and climate of the Madeira Islands and many of the islands of the South Seas are so favoured, and there the orange-trees are probably more at home than on any other portion of the earth's surface.

Another very apparent fact is that it luxuriates in land well endowed with fertility and moisture. In its nature in this respect it closely resembles the large-leaved and dark-foliaged scrub trees which clothe our mountain sides and glens and invariably find their home in a soil rich with humus, and where the roots can be always cool and moist. Where such scrub has thriven in Queensland the orange would thrive equally. Quite as apparent is the oft-repeated statement that a cold tenacious subsoil without natural drainage is, as nearly as possible, death to the trees. They want moisture, but it must be free from the poisonous gases and combinations which lurk in any soil where the air finds no access ; and hence want of proper drainage is anything but in keeping with Nature's laws or the requirements of these highly ornamental and valuable trees.

Following up Nature again, the fact confronts us that where our broad and dark-leaved scrub trees luxuriate there is not a vestige of weedy undergrowth to be found. Towards the boundaries of scrubs, where grasses and herbs appear, scrub trees cease to exist, and if any odd specimen shows under such conditions it tells its own tale of unthrift as a consequence of being surrounded with anything but fortuitous circumstances. In keeping with this it has frequently come to light of late years that where the marsupial scourge was worst, and grass and herbs were being worried out of existence, scrubs have started or been very much extended.

From these few facts a number of very important inferences bearing upon orange culture are fairly deducible. In the first place, too much must not be expected from them either in very hot or very cold situations. Then again, there is not sufficient reason for surprise if they fail to give satisfaction in a soil poorly charged with fertility. After a prolonged visitation of drought, again, it is not at all to be wondered at if they indicate waning vitality. The cultivator need not blame anyone but himself if they refuse to thrive in cold, sour, ill-drained land. And lastly, though not least, as this is not the age of miracles, he may expect failure who courts it by allowing any other surface crop, even of grass or other weeds, to occupy the land together with his orange-trees. Neglect of one or more of these hints or suggestions would prove to be the cause of many a failure, and should act as a caution to those who, with their eyes open to these facts, refuse to see them, and make an attempt to establish the industry in opposition to these necessary inferences.

It is necessary to remark just here that a large accumulation of facts at once assure the intended orange-grower that almost any kind of soil will favour the successful growth of the orange-tree, always provided that the natural laws are clearly apprehended and applied in practice when preparing the ground for its reception. Hard-and-fast rules can scarcely be laid down for the successful preparation of the land for orangeries, under the very widely differing circumstances of soil and climate throughout the length and breadth of the colony. No one can be told to do just so with the like certainty of success everywhere. The most and the best that can be done is to lay down broad and comprehensive principles which the intelligence of those interested must fairly grapple with so as to apply them in each case as differing circumstances may make necessary; and to the extent that this is done will be the measure of success realised.

IS THE ORANGE-TREE A SURFACE ROOTER?

It is generally understood that the orange-tree roots near the surface, but this is only partially true. Like many other half truths it tends to fatal consequences. It sends strong roots down into the subsoil as all large trees do, and consequently, when that subsoil is tenacious and sour, the roots therein start to die back, and simultaneously therewith the top does the same. And frequently the mischief does not end with the death of the tap-roots, for as death spreads upwards it soon seizes upon the surface roots, and then the trouble is past remedy. Orange-trees which have been lifted after failing have shown a strong system of vertical roots striking downwards in all directions from the surface horizontal ones, and when these penetrate into an unkindly substratum it quickly tells its tale in the waning luxuriance of the tree. The dark greenness is changed into a dingy brown or yellowish hue, dead wood appears, insects multiply, and the tree, if not already in its grave, will soon need to be removed to it. But it is nevertheless true that the bulk of the feeding roots of the orange-tree are near the surface, for they will be seen forming a thick mass of fibre in every direction, and on that account there should be no surface growth of any kind allowed to deprive the tree of the food and moisture it requires. This is a matter in connection with which too much ignorance, negligence, or unconcern is shown; and yet a few minutes' thought should satisfy any one that a tree requiring all the fertility and moisture it can possibly get (more especially in a very dry time), cannot possibly thrive when grasses and weeds are pumping up the moisture and thus robbing them of their necessary daily food. The practice so common, of allowing grass to grow thus, may also fairly be charged with much of the dying back to be seen in orangeries. When the surface roots are compelled to be inactive from the complete absence of any moisture for them to take up, the deeper roots will feel the strain and will put forth greater activity to preserve life; but in most instances, although they may find moisture, the elements of fertility will be wanting at their lower depths, and the most they can do, therefore, will be to foster a weak and mere lingering existence. While the tree is thus half-starved, and to that extent ailing and unhealthy, the many diseases and blights to which this valuable family of fruit trees is prone will be extremely likely to attack it and in its weak state obtain so decided an advantage over it that it will suffer almost beyond recovery. That such is the history, in brief, of many failures which meet the eye in the attempts at orange-growing is obvious, when, as is often seen, success and failure are found side by side, and in precisely the same circumstances of climate, soil, locality and aspect. It will easily be gathered from this that the writer earnestly advocates thoroughness in all matters of culture where the orange-tree is concerned, and it will now be necessary to speak more particularly with reference to this thoroughness.

PREPARING THE LAND.
DRAINING.

What preparation land may stand in need of for the reception of orange or any other trees depends upon several things, viz.—the nature of the soil and subsoil, the lay of the land generally, and whether it requires artificial drainage. This latter point each one will have to decide for himself, but a few general remarks will prove helpful in arriving at a decision. The question of drainage stands certainly first in importance, and any soil which will hold water for twenty-four hours after rain at the depth of 2 feet stands in need of under-drainage. When land is, by nature or otherwise, so thoroughly drained that all superfluous moisture percolates downwards as fast as it falls, it is all that could be desired in that particular for a*:* orangery. Let it be distinctly understood that want of drainage is not necessarily dependent upon the lay of the land. Some level flats are naturally well drained—that is, the subsoil cannot be made to hold water—while some hillsides, and steep at that, must be drained, as the subsoil is heavy and retains the water. In spite of all that has been said and absolutely proven by the greatest authorities of the day with reference to draining, notions which have been exploded, both by reason and repeated experiments, by showing that thoroughly drained land holds the moisture needful for healthy plant growth longer than undrained, this great and important underlying principle and truth is still largely regarded as a fallacy; and, if it were not that the mistakes consequent thereon often prove fatal, might be treated with the levity it deserves, and otherwise left unnoticed. But if orange-growing is ever to become a success in the land it must be otherwise. Scientific truths must be received and acted upon, and when that is fairly done proof of their general soundness will soon appear.

If, then, the subsoil at 2 feet below the surface is sufficiently retentive that it will hold water for twenty-four hours after rain, drains are absolutely necessary, or a failure is positively certain. Cause and effect are inseparable; Nature's laws are all alike, inviolable. When a man can put his hand into the fire without burning it there may be a probability of raising fruit profitably on ill-drained land. And just here—to make certain that no mistake shall arise at this important point—I will state with emphasis that the subsoil is more to be considered than the surface; for unless the subsoil is sound and healthful nothing that may be done with the surface can much mend matters.

With reference to drainage, experience has clearly shown that no underground drain should be laid shallower than 3 feet 6 inches or 4 feet, and the more rapidly the superfluous moisture can get away the less of the soluble elements of fertility are seized and carried away by it. Tiles are the best materials for making underground drains, and if a good job is intended they must be no more than from 18 to 20 feet apart. The most favourable position should be chosen for the tile drains to discharge into, which should be an open drain or ditch in the direction of the greatest fall. The tile branches should then be made to run diagonally—not at right angles to the main drain, but at an angle of, say, 45 degrees to it, and each to be parallel to the next throughout the plot or orchard. The tiles should be placed as close together as possible, and in soft ground a flat stone or piece of wood laid to catch the ends of each tile, or the one will be liable to sink out of the level of the other and cause a block in the drain. Clay should then be rammed around each joint firmly to make all tight and secure, and the water left to find its way to the tile from below, which it will do readily. Good serviceable drains can be, and are frequently, made with stones, wood, or other materials; but for durability and on the score of economy, where tiles can be had at all convenient'y, they are always preferable. When any other material is compulsory, make the drains with a clear open space down the centre to allow free course to the water. In any case make the drains as far away from the tree roots as possible, or they quickly make their way in great masses into the drains and choke them, thereby rendering them useless. Further particulars on this subject will be found in the earlier pages of the book.

TRENCHING.

But supposing that proper drainage is fairly secured, either naturally or artificially, the next thing is to know how the land may be best treated to promote healthy growth and fruitfulness. Bearing in mind that all the fertility possible is necessary with a regular supply of moisture, it follows that trenching or double-digging cannot be dispensed with, as both these important and valuable results are certainly to be attained thereby. Thus, preparing the land increases its fertility by aërating the soil to a greater depth, thereby mellowing and sweetening it; and also by giving all the worked portion a greater sponge-like capacity for gathering and storing moisture. The principles involved in the advocacy of trenching with thorough drainage have been forcibly illustrated in this climate already, the orange-tree in particular being the subject of the illustration. During several trying droughts of quite recent occurrence the writer of this essay has had orange-trees flourishing, making most vigorous growth and evidently feeling no ill effects from drought, and that without a particle of water being applied to them. The land in which they grew was naturally porous, so much so that it could not hold water for even one hour at any depth from 2 to 10 feet, being also hand trenched to the depth of 2 feet. Thus, it will be seen, is science borne out by practice, and it can be shown that notwithstanding the fact that the orange-tree is greedy of a full supply of moisture it can be grown successfully, even through a severe drought, without having recourse to irrigation. Not but what irrigation would be very helpful in an orangery; but seeing that it is costly and difficult to secure, let the labour of trenching be cheerfully accepted as a substitute, and no cause will be found for complaint. With said trenching, however, draining is absolutely imperative, and clean surface culture must also be ever maintained.

What is meant by trenching many will require to have made clear to them. In few words, it means breaking up the soil to the depth of 20 to 24 inches to let the air into it and increase its fertility, and at the same time increase its storage capacity for water. Practical men differ somewhat as to the best method of doing the work, but the majority favour the modern practice of leaving the top and bottom spits in the same position relatively as they were. Evidently this is Nature's method, and à priori should work most harmoniously with her laws; and those who have enjoyed the most and the widest experience in this matter assert themselves unmistakeably in its favour. Trenching—or "double-digging," as it is called—is done pretty much as follows:—Remove the surface spit from a strip of land of any required length, about 2 feet wide, depositing it as conveniently as possible to the spot where the work will terminate. Then, with a good strong steel digging-fork of the Parke's pattern, with tines from 12 to 14 inches in length, break up the second spit where it lies, mixing therewith meanwhile anything and everything that will tend to keep it open and porous, old corn cobs, megass from the sugar-mills, grass-tree stems broken up, cornstalks, old boots, brickbats, small rough stones, lime, rubbish, and the like. Some healthy and fruitful orange-trees, planted where the subsoil was strong soapy clay, were treated success-fully on this principle, the material used being logs, fully a dray-load being buried under each tree. When the second spit is thus broken up, and this rough opening material mixed with it, if any good manure is available, give the top a light dressing, and then proceed to mark out a second strip of equal dimensions with the first, and with the digging-fork break up the top spit, placing it on the top of the manure in the first trench, breaking it up well meanwhile. This done, the first trench is finished, and the remainder is to be done on the same principle, until the entire orangery or plot is completed With reference to the thorough pulverisation of the top spit, let it be faithfully attended to, especially in the immediate vicinity of where the tree is to be planted, but the second spit is none the better for being broken up so fine. With good tools a ready workman, in ordinary soil, will easily do from 1 rod to 1½ rods per day, and from 7s. 6d. to 10s. per rod is the price generally paid for it.

But some will ask, is there not a quicker and less costly method of breaking up the land which would be equally effectual? Yes; good work can be done with a plough and a strong team, if a plough capable of breaking up 12 inches of the surface is obtained, and a subsoil plough, drawn by a second team, follows in each open furrow, breaking up roughly an additional 6 or 7 inches. If these imple-ments are chosen to do the work, let the plot for the orangery be first thoroughly laid out with stakes to regulate the distance between the trees. Then start the ploughs down the centre of the row where the trees are to be planted, working the soil on either side towards the centre, finishing midway between each row with an open furrow. When the land is broken up to the required depth with both ploughs leave it a while to mellow, and then take the ordinary plough and go over it all again, working the soil again towards the centre on both sides so as to increase the ridge. To improve the work in removing inequalities and increasing the ridge yet further, let a good workman help the work with a long-handled shovel, throwing from the furrow to the crown of the ridge as necessary to regulate the work. Before planting the trees give the centre of each ridge a good harrowing with a long-toothed and heavy harrow, which, while pulverising the soil, will also tend to flatten the crown of the ridge, and then after staking the land it will be ready for the reception of the trees. If the site for the orangery is on the slope of a hill make the ridges and furrows as nearly as possible without any perceptible fall; and then in a dry time the little rain that falls will have no chance to get away without percolating downwards, and in the time of heavy rain it will have as little chance of swelling into an irresistible torrent. Storm channels will need to be provided in large orangeries at stated intervals, and always in unbroken land, to carry off surface water, so that it may have but little opportunity for carrying away the worked soil and thus making mischief. The same plan of forming an orangery into lands running in the direction where is the least fall on the sides of sloping hills may also be carried out to good purpose with hand-trenching if desirable, and in land at all heavy or strong, where drains are imperative, it is especially desirable that the covered drains be made along the lines of the furrows, not to carry off the storm waters, but the superfluous water contained in the tenacious subsoil.

SHELTER AND MULCH.

With reference to shelter, there are only a few localities in Queensland where it needs to be provided, and these are bleak exposed situations on the Downs and some other quarters where the full blast of our westerly winds is experienced and a strong degree of frost. Where the frost is nothing to speak of the orange-tree needs no shelter to keep off the cold, for the little it feels will help it rather than otherwise, and as we have no hot winds there is no necessity for providing shelter from them. Shelter from the sun's hottest rays would be desirable, but not in the form of any living shade-tree, and consequently it may be, or rather must be, left very severely alone. But there is one important matter of shade, both desirable and possible, which the orange-grower will require to provide for his young charges, and that is the shading of all the stems and branches, not omitting the main trunk, with healthy leafy wood. From the very first this needs to be considered, and it is more than probable that if the stems of young orange-trees were bandaged with grass or some such material it would prove to be very helpful to the tree as protection from the sun's rays, while it would also be a great check to the inroads of the coccus and scale which so terribly infest this class of plants. While trees are small it is an easy matter to shade them with boughs, but the shade must not be so dense as to exclude the light, only sufficient to break the intensity of the sun's severest heat. Shading of this description would no doubt be immensely serviceable to young orange-trees one or two years after planting.

Then there is another kind of shading or shelter which cannot be too strongly recommended, and that is the shading of the soil and, consequently, the roots of the orangery, with a good coating of mulch. The great benefit that results from keeping orchard land continuously mulched is not known as it deserves to be, or it would soon become a general practice. With deep trenching, efficient drainage, and a system of mulching carefully followed up, there would be little else to provide for to secure the greatest vigour and productiveness possible, and in every way the best results. One of the most promising orangeries to be seen anywhere in Queensland is circumstanced in every respect as above-mentioned. The soil is moderately fertile and deep, the drainage naturally perfect, and the proprietor finds that, by purchasing straw or some such material from the farmer to cover the entire surface of his orangery, his labour and cost of working it is thereby reduced to a minimum, for weeds make little work with mulch, and his yield is maintained at a maximum, for the mulch prevents any waste of moisture by evaporation. He also finds that as the mulch decomposes and turns into humus it supplies the bulk of the elements required to maintain the fertility of the soil, and where orangeries are within easy reach of a sugar-mill the megass would furnish an abundant supply of an excellent and serviceable mulch, the removal of which would be considered by many millowners as a great boon. Spent tanner's bark would also be a serviceable mulch for the orange-tree; but, on account of the length of time it requires to decompose, would hardly be equal to grass, straw, or megass.

ORANGE OR LEMON STOCKS.

If Queensland experience is to have its due weight in settling the vexed question relating to orange culture as to the best stock for oranges to grow upon, then the lemon stock cannot for one moment be countenanced as a satisfactory one for the orange-tree. In New South Wales this question is not definitely settled, and if any number of clear illustrations can be found to show that the orange does well on the lemon stock there they can show cause for continuing the use of the lemon stock. But it is not in my power to point out a single orangery in this colony, large or small, where the trees are growing on a lemon stock and to say that they are doing well.

It is, as a rule, understood that seedling orange-trees are in every way the best, and, in my opinion, this only squints at the truth, so to speak, for if the whole plain truth were known it would most likely be confirmative of the above—that the orange-tree is not sufficiently at home on the lemon stock to thrive. The facts of the case are that the bulk of the worked orange-trees, of any age in most orangeries, are on the lemon stock, and when seedling orange-trees are pitted against such they are known to be immensely more thrifty, enduring, and fruitful. But how do seedling oranges compare with orange-trees worked on an orange stock? My experience and observation go to prove that there is little if any difference between them, and the little that shows is rather in favour of the worked than the unworked stock. If in the same soil and treated well and similarly they are both satisfactory, the main if not the only difference between them being that the worked trees will invariably be first in coming into bearing. This, then, may be regarded as proof of a very satisfactory character that orange-trees require orange stocks to grow well upon, and it matters little whether they are seedlings or grafted if this is not overlooked. That the reader, however, may have a clear idea of the difference between the two, the worked orange often bears in two years after planting and very seldom goes beyond the third or fourth year. But a seedling may be five and as much as ten years before showing its fruit, and, as a rule, goes from six to seven years. Where immediate returns, then, are an object, worked trees are decidedly before seedlings, and so long as the stock is known to be the orange such may generally have the preference in the planting of an orangery.

PROPER PLANTING DISTANCE.

Having decided with reference to the preparation of the soil and other matters incidental thereto, and also as to the proper stock for the orange to grow on, the distance necessary to plant the trees apart next requires settlement. On this important point there are wide differences of opinion, and at least a show of reason is given on both sides. Some contend that an orangery is best cultivated after Nature's method, in a thick scrub the trees all near enough to each other to thoroughly shade the soil and so preserve an equable temperature therein. The object aimed at is undoubtedly good, if it could be attained without injuring the tree in other respects, and if that object could not be accomplished otherwise. But we have already shown that, by a good coating of mulch, this important end may be realised, so that it is not essential at all events; and it is by no means difficult to show that close planting is neither more nor less than a suicidal policy.

In the first place, we must take into consideration the average rainfall in connection with the wants of each individual tree; and, on the well-known mechanical principle that nothing is stronger than its weakest point, it is actually the wants of each tree during a season of drought that should alone settle the question. What has to be decided, therefore, is whether land thinly or thickly planted will hold its moisture longest. Many would at once say that there should be no difference of opinion on that score; nor should there be, but, unfortunately, there is, and if the majority of cultivators expressed an opinion it would be decidedly the reverse of fact. There are some intelligent cultivators who frame their conclusions only when they have the whole of the facts of the case before them, but, unfortunately they are only few; the bulk of them jump at conclusions from insufficient premises, and consequently are caught by a fallacy. In deciding this matter the majority only take into account the action of the sun's rays upon the soil and the evaporation that follows, and from such premises conclude that if a crop can be made to cover the ground, the sun's power is lost—or, at least, reduced to a minimum upon it. But a very important premise is lost sight of in such reasoning, and that is the evaporation going on through the foliage of the growing plant. The functions of the roots are to pump up the moisture from the soil together with soluble fertilising materials and these are then forwarded to the leaves to be aërated; and as the air is utilised for the assistance it is required to give, the moisture escapes through innumerable leaf pores in exact proportion to the heat of the weather and the vigour of growth in the plant. The evaporation which actually takes place in the leaf as exposed to the sun is very

D

simply illustrated by separating the leaf from the tree and noting the result. As a matter of fact, we all know it quickly parts with its moisture and wilts or shrivels up. The only difference between this severed leaf and those left on the growing plant is, the latter are supplied with moisture as rapidly as they lose it, and this being the case, the more foliage a tree has, and the longer and broader it is, the more opportunity there is for the evaporation of moisture. Apply this to the orange-tree and what is the result? Being a tree which in health carries a wealth of broad leaves, their surfaces, containing innumerable pores, must be the seat of great activity in the matter of evaporation when the temperature of the atmosphere ranges high. This goes on in every case, whether the ground is shaded or not, and with millions of small rootlets acting as pumps below ground, and an immense amount of evaporating surface exactly proportionate with the leaf surface above, moisture cannot hold out long when land is crowded. Facts in other departments of cultivation prove this view of matters to be correct. Maize, when grown thickly for fodder purposes, will not remain vigorous during even a short spell of dry weather, while maize sown thinly for grain will grow and ripen its crop with much less than half the rainfall necessary to keep the fodder crop growing. The reason is the latter exposes a greater surface of foliage to the atmosphere, and the moisture evaporates the quicker, although the soil is densely shaded. And without going further than the orangery for an illustration, it will have been noticed that when drought prevails the leaves of the orange-trees often curl up and lose their freshness during the heat of the day and recover themselves partially again during the night. The reason is the roots cannot collect enough moisture from the earth while evaporation is at its highest during the day, and the leaves show it; but during the night, as the evaporation decreases, the circulating sap helps to recovery. So, then, the point where evaporation is always and obviously greatest is not from the soil, but the leaves, through the influences and action of sun heat. Over this the cultivator has no control except what is afforded him by thin planting. Fewer trees with less leaf surface will cause less evaporation; and as the supply of moisture below is at once effectually saved from waste by mulching, as already noticed, it becomes perfectly clear that the best way to make the annual rainfall serve the wants of the orange-tree and its valuable crop, the trees must not be allowed to overcrowd the land, or the one must stint and starve the other altogether beyond remedy. My experience and observation is entirely in support of this view, for during seasons of drought splendid crops of oranges have been gathered from trees having plenty of room for roots and top, nothing occupying the land between; while trees that have been crowded have thrown their entire crop. The only safe course to follow, therefore, is to plant sufficiently wide so that the trees may have a chance of doing reasonably well during a season of drought; for if they can be regarded as safe or nearly so for a dry and trying season they are sure to be all right in a good one. Bearing upon this point directly, and the more to enforce it, I will cite a fact which has attracted considerable attention among the orchards in America. There it has been noticed that the outside rows of trees in orchards, or single rows, and also single trees, are invariably more healthy, more fruitful, and more enduring than those planted in the body of an orchard, and the obvious and necessary inference to be drawn from such facts is that this is the natural result of having more room. But again, if the trees are crowded scrub-fashion it always follows that the fruit is limited to those branches which have proper access to the vivifying and ripening influences of light and air, and in overcrowded orchards, as also in scrubs, these are only the uppermost branches. In no sense can this be deemed desirable, for a full crop cannot be gathered under such circumstances, and what there is is anything but convenient to gather. The orange-tree, therefore, to do its best, should have room all round it for the light and air to act, and when that is the case there will be good walking space all round between each tree. A tree so grown, with its wealth of golden fruit bearing down its branches on every side, would be a pleasing picture indeed to look upon, as it is a very worthy object to plan and provide for. Taking it for granted, therefore, that plenty of room is exceedingly desirable for the orange, the question what is plenty has next to be decided.

Judging from the orangeries now to be seen in Queensland, 20 feet space between each tree is not plenty. In some exceptional and extreme cases experienced men are leaving as much as 30 feet by 40 feet space for their orange-trees; but it is almost overdoing it if the land is intended to be kept for oranges alone. If the land is to be utilised for growing other crops between the trees such space is none too much. An orangery, however, should not be an orangery and something else. A crop of oranges is quite enough to take from the land every year if proper economy is studied. Burning the candle at both ends is not to be recommended in any case. If it is made a question whether the land between the trees shall be cultivated partially with a crop for a few years or woefully neglected, it would be best to try the cultivation on the principle of choosing the least of two evils, but not otherwise. With reference to distance, from 25 to 30 feet apart may be considered a proper thing in good and well-prepared land; and in such, with regular care and timely attentions, they will soon occupy the whole of it, leaving only walking space between.

PRUNING THE TREES.

Another necessary part of orange culture is the pruning, and the very nature of this operation makes it of the utmost importance that it be done in strict accordance with the requirements of the tree or left severely alone. Pruning, although not, strictly speaking, natural, must not become unnatural. It cannot too often be called to mind that we cannot mend or bend Nature, but we may assist her. Pruning when judiciously done helps Nature. Like every other tree brought into cultivation by man the orange-tree is the better for a little pruning. Uncultivated trees—that is, trees in a complete state of nature—frequently show dead limbs, which is Nature's way of getting rid of an encumbrance. Intelligent pruning anticipates this somewhat, and severs a spent limb or branch before it becomes unsightly. Nature always strives in some way to preserve a proper balance in the tree, and the intelligent pruner renders her valuable assistance. Nature again sends out branches laden with foliage in every direction to the light and free air, so that they may be acted upon by the elements and made fruitful; and the observant pruner, having a clear understanding of the why and the wherefore of his work, aims to assist Nature at this as at every other point. It should be distinctly understood that pruning is necessarily subject to certain laws, and cannot be done to any advantage by chance or haphazard. The object of pruning fruit-bearing trees is to increase the bearing capabilities of the trees without sacrificing the general health, vigour, or appearance. With these broad and general principles laid down, it is necessary to consider a few particulars.

In the first place, then, unless there are strong indications of failing vigour in a tree, excessive pruning should be avoided. The natural tendency of using the knife too freely is to induce a strong growing woody habit, and thus perpetuate the excess which needed checking. The safe rule in all pruning is to cut vigorous growing trees as little as possible and to use the knife with the greatest freedom where the making of new strong wood is a necessity. Trees making strong watery shoots have an excess of roots over top, and if pruned in accordance with indicated requirements will be pruned below the ground and not above. Trees barely making an inch or two of young wood in a season have either too little root or insufficient nourishment to make progress, or they may have inherited an impaired and a weakly constitution, in which case they are best pruned (or rather pulled) out altogether; but where the stunting is merely accidental heavy pruning is not only admissible, for it is desirable. At the same time, the proprietor should see that some good fertiliser is applied to the tree to help it into a better—that is, a more vigorous and fruitful—state; but the application of fertilising matter should be to the extreme feeding points of the roots, outside the diameter of the branches, and not, as is frequently the case, close round about the stem.

The style of pruning suited to the nature of the orange-tree is more of a general thinning out than a cutting back. This tree bears on the ripened twigs at the points of the branches, and in all cases a sufficiency of these must be left to give a crop of fruit. An occasional limb will need to be sawn clean out at times, where the chafing of two together is manifest or the tree is excessively crowded; but when this is done nothing in the shape of a stump should be left to die back, or eventually it will extend further and cause adjoining limbs to die back also. One other thing must also be observed in pruning the orange-tree: the wood must be left on all sides to shade the limbs and stem as much as possible. Some of the most experienced orange-growers in the world say that this is a very important safeguard against disease and decay in the tree.

When the vigour of the top is such as to indicate that root pruning is necessary it should be done by cutting a trench a foot or so wide all round the tree at the circle of the outer branches to the depth of 2 feet, or as low down as the roots are found. But the best of pruning for the orange as well as every other fruit tree is what is called "finger-and-thumb pruning." This is done at the opposite season to the general pruning, and is therefore also called "spring and summer pruning." It is at once both simple and easy, and consists in pinching off with finger and thumb all shoots that are misplaced and uncalled for wherever they may appear. Doing this saves the tree from wasting its energies in making wood which would require to be afterwards removed with the knife. In conclusion, then, let it be understood that an orange-tree, when properly pruned, will not be at all open—at any rate not sufficiently so to see through it; and in this respect it differs from many other equally useful fruit trees.

MANURING.

To cultivate the orange successfully it must be artificially fertilised, but not necessarily with what are known as "artificial manures." At an earlier stage in this essay mulching is recommended, the decomposed mulch to be dug in from time to time and more applied afresh. If this is regularly attended to a falling off in the vigour and fruitfulness of the tree will scarcely be possible; still an occasional dressing with bone dust or decomposed stockyard or stable manure will be all that is required to maintain proper fertility in the soil and necessary health and vigour in the tree. Guano and other similar stimulants are known to be useful in a limited degree, but those who have had the most experience with them the most readily express doubts as to their value. The liquid excrements of animals are of special value as a fertiliser to the orange tree, and also the ammoniacal liquor from the gasworks, if very freely diluted, say, with one part of the liquor to 100 or even more parts of water. Wood-ashes and lime are also particularly serviceable, and some orange-trees in this colony have shown immense vigour and fruitfulness when dressed with wood-ashes alone. But after all the question of manuring must be decided by the nature and requirements of the soil in which the trees are planted. Soils are of various and uncertain qualities, and therefore no hard-and-fast rules can be laid down for their enrichment. There is, however, one very safe rule to observe in the treatment of the orange with reference to this matter, and that is to burn nothing in the shape of weeds or any other vegetable matter which can in any way be returned otherwise. Humus, or decomposed vegetable matter, is what this tree loves, and burning destroys it, and if followed up—as is the case in some instances—continuously tends, and that certainly, to the rapid exhaustion of the soil.

ORANGE PESTS.

There is yet one other matter compelling attention to ensure success in orange culture, and that is " How can it be successfully freed from its many insect foes ?" Although this may be the last it is by no means the least of the attentions this valuable fruit tree requires at our hands. Most fruit trees have their one pest to harass them at times; but this one in most instances has almost a legion of them always, and it is a question of the utmost importance how to overcome them. No doubt systematic and thorough cultivation is a very great safeguard against the attacks of parasites or disease, but it is not in every respect an infallible remedy or preventive. With all the care and attention possible, the insect foes, which everywhere abound, will make a desperate effort to establish themselves. With reference to their dislodgment, it is always advisable to attack them as soon as possible after they first appear. In one particular they are much the same as weeds, which, if left to run to seed, are no sooner cut down and killed than a fresh crop shows, and if these are again promptly levelled it is again and again repeated. So with insects when left long enough to breed. The first batch is no sooner destroyed than the second hatches, and when that is destroyed the third will follow. Promptness, therefore, in applying a sufficient remedy is the first consideration; for let a nostrum be ever so sufficient its results can only be partial when the enemy has had sufficiently long possession of the tree. With reference to the best remedies, there are several very good, and one of the oldest in use is soft soap, sulphur, and chloride of lime, a tablespoonful of each to a gallon of water, the soft soap and sulphur to be incorporated by boiling and the chloride of lime stirred in when cold. This mixture is best applied with a syringe when fairly hot, and requires to be driven with force among the branches so as to thoroughly wet every portion where the scale has effected a lodgment. This, although a good proved remedy, is objected to by many because it is extremely liable to injure the crop of fruit, and, if used at all stronger than above recommended, it will also kill some of the young wood and foliage.

Some who have experience of this remedy, and have also used boiling water, say that the latter is in every respect preferable; for while it is thoroughly efficient in killing the scale and other insect pests it will not injure the tree in any way. Although the writer of this has never personally used boiling water for the purpose, he has seen several orangeries where it is always relied on, and it never fails to render the service required of it without in any way injuring the tree. Testimony, therefore, is more in favour of the boiling-water cure than the soft-soap and sulphur one.

But another general insecticide is fast coming into notice and favour, and that is kerosene, made soluble in water. James Pottie, veterinary surgeon, in Sydney, recently made known, through the columns of *Casiner's Monthly*, that he had discovered how to make kerosene soluble in water. This mineral oil had frequently proved valuable as an insecticide previously, but the plants in most of the cases suffered almost as much, so that the remedy was quite as bad as the disease. It was proved that no expedient would allow of kerosene and water mixing, and the oil alone would kill plants readily. But the problem is now solved, and kerosene is made soluble in water as follows:—In a common washing-copper boil 4 gallons of water, 1 lb. of soft-soap, and 4 ozs. of washing-soda until thoroughly mixed. Then add a pint and a-quarter of kerosene, and stir freely until the mixture is of a uniform consistency. To this should be added 12 gallons of water, making it 16 gallons in all. A dose may be applied by means of a fine syringe, wherever the presence of a single insect marauder is observed. This is pretty sure to become a very popular, as it is a very cheap, remedy.

Notwithstanding the expressed value of the last-named insecticide, it would be a serious omission to leave out the *pyrethrums*. Nothing is appearing to give more general or complete satisfaction in the destruction of insects of every name than the various insect powders prepared from the dried flowers of *pyrethrum carneum*. In America, where it has been made plentiful and cheap by cultivation, it has been applied with great success in quite a variety of ways—in the dry powder sprinkled upon the insects or burnt in a close place where they abound, and also by making it into a decoction or a tincture. In some of these forms, presumably in the two last-mentioned, it will be found serviceable in the destruction of our minute and innumerable orange parasites.

The Californian scale of all kinds is removed from the orange-tree by spraying them with a solution of whale-oil soap. The result is the fruit is generally clear and bright in the skin and is not injured in the least. Two sprayings are found necessary to effectually clean the tree. The whale-oil soap water in its operation seems to kill the insect, the smut rising in a crust from the fruit by the action of the sun and wind, and gradually flaking off. The solution as used is something like three-fourths of a pound of the soap to a gallon of water. This is said to be much better than sulphur, as it leaves the fruit beautifully clean and does not clog the syringe as does the sulphur.

The latest idea mooted with reference to these orange pests is that they succeed in their work of injuring the trees simply because they are lacking in "life force." The originator of this idea is a practical man—none other than James Pottie, veterinary surgeon, of New South Wales—and he has such faith in it that he asks volunteers to aid him in proving it; and wanting that, he proposes trying for himself. May he be successful is my wish; and as he is very unlikely to give expression to any crude theory there is much probability of good resulting from his experiments.

THE CITRUS FAMILY.

Before concluding this short essay, an interesting and useful chapter may be added with reference to the various useful members of this family. The treatment recommended is intended for all alike, for although there are natural differences between them they are sufficiently alike in character to be so treated.

There is first the European orange (*Citrus aurantium*), with its many well-known varieties, and which as a dessert fruit is the highest in popular estimation. Any nurseryman's catalogue will give a descriptive list of one and all of them, which need not therefore be given here. Then there is the mandarin (*Citrus nobilis*), with its many favourites, with which all are familiar. Both these members of this large family are deserving of extended and better culture.

Then there is the head of the family, the citron (*Citrus medica*), which came originally from the warm parts of Asia. This is also useful for its peel and its juice, and an essential oil is extracted by expression from its rind called the oil of citron, used to give aroma and flavour to liqueurs and sweetmeats. Of these there are several varieties.

Then there is the lime (*Citrus limetta*), in many respects bearing a close resemblance to the lemon-tree, except that everything is smaller. The West India lime has the reputation of being best for limejuice, which, by the way, is an exceedingly useful commodity, and should be freely used as an antidote to scorbutic affections in every country. There are several varieties of this also.

The lemon is the fruit of (*Citrus limonum*), which has also gone into many varieties. The peel and the juice, together with the citric acid and the oil of the peel, are the principal marketable commodities obtained from it.

The shaddock (*Citrus decumana*) is the last, and at the same time the least known, member of the family. Some varieties are esteemed for preserving, and the red-fleshed is noted for keeping well and carrying where few others of the family are obtainable.

Many of these fruit trees are rated below their real value as economical plants. The flowers distilled supply orange-flower water, a well-known perfume. The flowers of the Seville orange are largely used for this purpose in Italy and France. An oil, called *Neroli*, is also obtained by distillation from them, and the popular Eau de Cologne largely owes its peculiar perfume to its presence. In the dried state orange peel is a mild tonic and carminative, and is often used in combination with bitter herbs and barks, such as gentian, Peruvian bark, and colombo, in making infusions or tinctures. A delicious wine is also made from the orange, and the beverage known as orangeade.

Lemons and limes are mostly valued for their juice, and an allusion has already been made to its value. It is known to be cooling, and properly diluted is a useful beverage for free use during summer or in some forms of inflammatory fevers; and of late drinking the pure juice of the lemon and lime has been highly extolled as a remedy against severe attacks of rheumatism and gout.

Now, although these and many other valuable commodities are yielded by this family, the only uses they are at present applied to are the oranges for dessert and the lemons for flavouring beverages and in culinary requirements. Our peel is not candied, our flowers not distilled, the oil of the orange, lemon, and citron is not expressed, and all our citric acid and limejuice are imported. The ruling prices of these things in the colonies are 12s. per lb. for the oil of lemon, 2s. per lb. for orange-flower water, 1s. per lb. for candied peels, 3s. for citric acid, and for the oil of orange-bloom 12s. per ounce. America is looking after these things, as the following extract from the *Scientific American* will show:—" England formerly monopolised our market for citric acid to the extent of 250,000 lbs. annually at 1 dollar 30 cents. per lb., while last year only 27,000 lbs. were imported and sold at the same rate as the American product—57 cents. per lb."

Clearly the citrus family may be made to do more for us than it is doing; but in the meantime we must try and do more for it, and that this essay may help on the good work is the wish of the author.

LABOR OMNIA VINCIT.

HINTS TO NEW-COMERS.

BY PRICE FLETCHER.

[NOTE.—These papers first appeared in the *Queenslander*, during the year 1879. There have been so many inquiries as to whether they were re-published as a separate pamphlet that we have arranged with the Author for permission to insert them in these pages.—ED.]

AMONG our new arrivals there are always a certain number who have left the old country with the intention of getting a piece of land really their own, on which they can make a home for themselves—may be, get married, and settle down. I am happy to be able to tell them that in this fine colony they can, by patiently persevering, do that, and have no fear of landlord or tax-collector before their eyes; a state of happy content utterly beyond the possibility of an agricultural labourer in any European country whatever. In this paper I intend to try and give such hints as may, perhaps, be of use to those who are strangers to our climate, our woods, and method of cultivation. Also, I will try and show that any man who will keep sober, and be frugal and industrious, will, in the long run, be successful.

I will leave, for the present, immigrants who come out here with some capital and experience in farming at home, and will suppose you (the reader) are a young man who lands here without money or friends, but with good health and strength, and who are determined to succeed. Before entering on the practical part of my paper, I would just counsel you not to give way to the feeling of "home sickness," which you will doubtless experience. It will pass away as soon as you get to know a few folks, and after you have been here twelve months, instead of wishing, as you no doubt have done, " that you had never come to such a wretched country," you will find yourself thinking how you can get over your brother or sister, or, may be, the old folks also. At any rate, remember this: that if, after a fair trial, you find the colony not to your liking, you or any man can, in half-a-year, save enough money to take passage home again.

The first thing you should do is to hire on to some farm or station. Never mind about high wages for a beginning; take the first reasonable offer, and so make a start in your new life. After a time, if you find anything objectionable in your employer, why, this is a free land, and you can leave him. But I would here give you a word of advice: do not be too proud to be found fault with—that is the great failing of most men who have been some years in the colonies. I do not counsel servileness, but only due forbearance, for you should remember that every employer likes to have his own way in his own affairs (it will be the same with you by-and-bye); and also remember that every one at times is found fault with, from even the manager to the labourer. Civility and sobriety go a great way with all masters, and cover a multitude of sins in the way of inefficiency or slowness, but they do not compensate for laziness; nothing puts a master's back up so much as that! I cannot too strongly inculcate the necessity for your learning every department of bush handicraft that you can possibly get the chance of learning. If your employer asks if you can do so-and-so, and you cannot, say you cannot; but say, also, that you doubtless soon could if he would show you how; and then try; and, however awkward it is, yet stick to it. Learn to milk, break in heifers, drive bullocks and horses, put up fences, sink wells, stock-ride, and slaughter; do your best to learn the use of tools, especially the axe, adze, saw, and maul and wedges. If you have hired to a squatter you can learn all this work on a station; and if it is a sheep station you can also learn *to shear*. I put great stress on this latter point, for whenever you come to select—having no capital but what you have saved—by being a good shearer you can every year earn, in three or four months, enough to keep your selection going for the rest of the year; so make it a point to ask your employer to let you be at work about the shearing shed; you will thus get an insight into the matter, and, at odd times, may have the chance of getting hold of a sheep which a shearer has already "opened up," or begun; and so next year, when you ask your employer to let you learn to shear, it will not then be such awkward work. I really do not know a more awkward, and, at first, difficult work for a beginner than this shearing—especially to a long-backed man; but perseverance will do wonders. Keep steadily at it, work slowly, try and get a good style; never mind about making a big cheque the first season or two, but remember that in learning to shear you are actually learning a new trade, by which you can always earn a living in any Australian colony. After two seasons you will find yourself wondering how you could call it difficult; your shears will slip through easily, and you will earn money by it.

  I may as well tell you now that, if you do as the majority of shearers and bushmen do when they get their cheques—that is, to go to the first public-house and " knock it down "—you will, like this " majority of bushmen," ever remain a bushman, and never rise to be an employer;

so when you are paid put the money in the Savings Bank. It will be quite safe, for the Government guarantee it, and you will get 5 per cent. interest on it yearly. If there is no Savings Bank branch near you, then ask your employer to open an account in your name by letter; or, better still, do it yourself. All you have to do is to write to the Colonial Treasurer, Savings Bank Department, Brisbane, enclosing your cheque and your name, employment and address, and by return post the bank sends you an acknowledgment and a book. You can draw it out whenever you like, at any branch office, or by letter. Remember that it will only be by your saving every shilling that you will be able to acquire enough to select a piece of land.

The next accomplishment that will most likely come in useful to you as a selector is that of bullock-driving; though, unless you are a very young man, you are not likely ever to be able to acquire the skill and style of a colonial-born driver, still you may easily gain skill enough to be able to drive the home-station team, and so be able, when the time comes, to do your own driving when clearing and breaking up your selection. In fact, the selector who owns a team of bullocks and can drive them is in a better position than many of his neighbours who have capital. Another reason why I urge you to qualify yourself for this peculiarly colonial calling is, that a good bullock-driver can always, if steady, be certain of good wages; so that if things go wrong with you on your selection you still have (like the shearer) a trade to fall back upon, and also that, as your time need not be all taken up on your farm, if you have a team of bullocks you can for some months in the year do a little in carrying goods or wool for the neighbouring storekeeper or station, and so help to bring money enough in to keep your wife and little ones while the crops are growing. The same remarks apply to horse-driving; but to the new selector bullocks are by far the best.

There is another thing you must also do your best to learn, although it is not likely you will ever be able to take to it as a trade; I mean slaughtering. Learn to kill and dress quickly and neatly both sheep and cattle. In the old country you might live a lifetime and never require the knowledge, but in the colonies it is very different. You will have a chance during your two years of station life to get a good insight into this matter, and when you have your own home and your own cattle you will find this skill will be invaluable to you; also, you may then very likely have opportunities of selling some of your meat among your neighbours or to travellers, and so earn a little in that way; but badly-dressed and badly-cured meat no one will buy if he can help. The risk you run through this same badly-killed meat spoiling in this hot climate is also very great.

If you have been a farm labourer at home you will probably know how to milk; if you do not you must not lose any opportunity you may have of learning. It is an awkward and disagreeable thing for a beginner, and is best learned when young; but as you are looking forward to being yourself the owner of cows, the necessity for your learning does not need to be dwelt upon by me. If you are not a farm labourer, and do not know how to plough, sow, mow, or reap, you are not likely to be able to learn how to do those things on a squatting station; there is nothing of this sort goes on till the land is sold, such as is the case about the Darling Downs.

Although I speak of your remaining two years on a squatting station, you must not run away with the idea that you will have been able to have saved enough to enable you to select in that short time; it will take you from five to ten years of steady work—no extravagance, but on the contrary careful saving—before you will have money enough to venture with. But you need not lose heart; Queensland is very big, and good land is in superabundance. You will always be able to get land, so do not fret yourself and be in a hurry. I am supposing you to be a young man now: if by the time you are thirty-five you have managed to acquire a good bullock or horse team, dray, &c., and have a nice selection of some hundreds of acres, you will be in a better position than ninety-nine out of every one hundred persons you meet. Many of the large Queensland sheep farmers, with whom the getting of their wool to port is a difficulty, very often give to a sober industrious man a team of bullocks, and allow him to work it out by his contracting to carry for them a certain quantity of wool every year. This is a chance which it is quite possible for you to get; also, you may, by attention to your work, rise to be overseer, and so get double wages; or many other little chances may crop up, so that by the end of the time I mention your savings will be greater than you may suppose possible when you only look at the amount of your yearly wages.

If, after you have been about two years on a station, you see no likelihood of such chances as I have just mentioned ever cropping up, although you have gained the name of a good steady man, then I should advise you to travel and see a little more of the country. Travelling out here costs very little; all you want is an old horse and saddle, and then you can carry your blankets, &c. A very little money buys flour, meat, tea, and sugar, and you are as independent as a king, can go where and what distance you like, or camp at the nearest water and best grass. It is astonishing what information you pick up by even only seeing other districts and other ways of doing things. But I do not mean you to be an idle traveller; you should take a job of sheep washing here, shearing there, splitting, fencing, or any other work;

and also by all means then go into the farming districts and get work there, so as to learn the special modes of our farming, and somewhat of the seasons for putting in crops, &c. You must now seize the opportunity of learning to plough, sow, mow, reap, and to do other farm work. Even if you were a farm labourer at home, and knew how to do all these things, yet you will find that you have much to learn : farming is so different out here to what it is in the old country. After you have spent some time—say another two years—travelling and at odd jobs, and have got somewhat sick of it, I would then counsel you to settle down in the neighbourhood which you like best, or in which you are best known as a steady man and a good worker—say the station you first went to. You will now be no "new chum," but will be able to earn a good living, for you will be up in many things; you can shear, or take station contracts for fencing, splitting, erecting huts, well-sinking, dam-making, &c. Although you may not get all this on the one place, you must remember that the fame of a good worker and steady man soon travels from station to station, and you would not be likely to find work slack.

You ought now to have a tidy little sum to your credit in the savings bank. As you only have interest allowed up to £200, I would advise you to always keep that amount there as a "nest egg," and any surplus you may get you can invest in cattle, if you have won the confidence of your employer sufficiently to be allowed to let them graze on his run—or take payment in cattle instead of in cash, if you can. A large proportion of the now richest squatters of Victoria and New South Wales were at one time only shepherds and stockmen; but in the early days it was a very common usage for them to be paid their wages in stock, to which they stuck, and at the present time they are our wealthiest men.

Presuming that now you will be inclined to get a nice young wife and start housekeeping and farming on your own account, I will give such practical details from a long personal experience in the colonies, as I think may be useful to you; commencing with the way in which you will have to proceed in the selecting of your land.

In the former pages my "hints" were confined entirely to the case of a young man without capital, but many of our immigrants are possessed of considerable capital, and come with the intention of immediately settling on land; they, also, may perhaps find a little information in my papers. I would strongly counsel such men not to be in a hurry to choose their land; no matter whether their capital be only a few hundreds or up to a few thousands, it will be greatly to their advantage to delay, and learn something of the peculiarities of our strange climate. In the case of a man who has only a few hundreds, I should say to him, "Bank your money and take a situation"; and to the richer sort, if too proud to do this, then I should counsel a whole year's travelling, not only in a steamboat from port to port, but inland on horseback, from district to district, from station to farm. Join as a volunteer a travelling mob of cattle, stay some time on a sheep farm or station, visit the sugar-growing localities, and gather information from all sources; for, as sure as ever you invest without first thoroughly acquainting yourself with what you are going into, you will rue it—remember, it is cheaper to learn experience from another than at your own expense.

Queensland offers every range of situation and climate, so you can choose for yourself whether you will settle in the cool districts of our southern mountainous land, where European fruits and vegetables grow easily and to perfection, or whether you will go into our tropical north, where the more delicate but more luxuriant tropical productions thrive well. I will suppose, however, that you want to know something of how, where, and at what price, you can get land. I shall not enter too fully into all the minutiæ of our Land Acts, but just give you such preliminary information as will enable you to know how to seek and get your selection.

First, as to where you can select. All Queensland is not open for anyone to go and pick out a piece of land, but from time to time large districts are proclaimed open, and you can take up your block anywhere in those districts; this proclamation is made in the *Government Gazette*, and is also fully made known by all the metropolitan and the local papers, so that there is no likelihood of your not knowing it. Then, if you go to the nearest land-office, you can get maps of the district, and also the officials will give you every information. You need not fear want of courtesy in any Queensland land-office.

Any person can select (whether newly arrived or not) who is eighteen years or more of age, whether man or woman, excepting married women. There are different classes of land you can select, namely:—(1.) Grazing Farms: Under the Act of 1884 you can take up land for this purpose, to the large quantity of 20,000 acres, but you cannot take less than 2,560 acres. The annual rent is fixed by the proclamation, but is never less than $\frac{3}{4}$d. per acre. Your selection must be fenced in during the first three years, or a lease will not be granted. If the fencing conditions are fulfilled, however, a lease for 30 years will issue. (2.) Agricultural Farms may also be taken up in quantities varying from 320 acres to 1,280 acres. These must be fenced in during the first five years, and then a lease for 50 years will issue; or they may be purchased at the end of ten years, at £1 per acre, or more, as circumstances at the time of application may suggest. There is one condition which you have to fulfil in respect of both classes of selections viz. :—Continuous and *bonâ fide* residence, either by yourself or by a bailiff in your employ—a copy of your agreement with your bailiff (if you do not personally reside) must be lodged and registered at the land-office. (3.) If you are willing to be contented with a small area of land which you mean to farm yourself, you can get it much more cheaply than in the previous cases by selecting what is called a "Homestead." This is an agricultural farm, the area of which must not exceed 160 acres. If at any time before the end of seven years from the commencement of the time of the lease you prove to the Commissioner of Crown Lands that you have for five years continuously and honestly resided on the land *yourself* (no bailiff or substitute is here allowed), and that you have spent ten shillings per acre in substantial and permanent improvements, such as houses, fences, wells, clearings, gardens, cultivation, and so forth, then you can acquire the freehold at once by payment of a sum of money which when added to the rent already paid will amount to 2s. 6d. per acre, together with the ordinary deed fees. So that after five years the land is your own, if you have fulfilled the necessary conditions.

Your rent is due on the 31st of March in every year; if you do not pay it then you are allowed to let it run on for 90 days of the same year, but in that event you have also to pay a fine in some cases as high as 15 per cent. of the annual rent. If you do not pay before the expiration of 90 days, then you will forfeit the land and all improvements. If it can be proved against you that you have failed to fulfil the conditions of occupation or residence your lease will be forfeited.

I will suppose you have decided on what land you want to select; so I will tell you what next to do. Get two, or three, as the case may require, of the printed forms of "application"; these will be given you gratis on asking for them at any land-office, and you can also be there shown how to fill them up. On these applications you must put a clear description of the locality and boundaries of your selection, and also state if it is surveyed or not. These applications have to be signed and sworn before some magistrate; that is, you take oath that you are of the full age of eighteen years, that you select the land for your own use, and that you are entitled to select; then you lodge them at the land-office, and at the same time deposit one full year's rent, together with the survey fee. The survey fee varies, according to the size of your block, from 12s. for one acre, and gradually diminishing *pro rata* till for 640 acres you only have to pay £8, and after that, for every 640 acres or fraction of 640 acres, you pay £4 additional.

On lodging your application you will be told when the land court will be held, and if you do not attend, in person or by your duly authorised attorney, the application will be rejected, and you will have a fine of 20s. deducted from your deposit money; the rest will be refunded. The Commissioner will declare in open court whether your application is accepted or not. The land agents give receipts for all moneys paid by applicants.

There are other clauses in the Act dealing with death, insolvency, transfers, mortgages, deeds of grant, &c., &c., but these do not come within my province to write about. I have mentioned all that is necessary for you, the newly-arrived farmer, to at present understand.

Never select land without first seeing it and judging its capabilities for yourself.

As to the locality you should choose for your home.—Even if you are a man without capital, if you have but experience in colonial ways (as fully spoken of previously), then you may venture to take up a small homestead; but you must be sure to take it in a locality where you *can get work* easily; *this is absolutely necessary for your success*, for you must remember that personal residence for the five years is imperative. If you have a wife and family, and they reside with you on it, you can of course be absent when at your work, and it does not mean that you cannot go away driving a dray, or shearing, or reaping, &c., but you must virtually reside—that is, *make it your home*.

It is as well for you to be reminded, before you take your selection, that, if your block adjoins any other person's selection, you will have to fence your half of the boundary fence between you within six months' time, if he gives you notice to that effect; or, if you do not do it, then he can fence it for you and charge you half of what it cost; so calculate your expenses before you select, and do not take too large a block, for fencing is very expensive. Many a selector has been crippled in pocket for years by this heavy outlay for fencing. If your neighbour is a rich man you may perhaps be able to make some such arrangement as for him to find the material and you the labour; but of course any such arrangement as that depends upon the nature of the country you have got, for there is far more labour in putting up a fence of split stuff than one of wire, so that what would be an equal agreement in one district would not be so in another. But I am supposing that you have made yourself sufficiently acquainted with colonial ways not to get the worst of a mutual agreement like the above.

I will say nothing about the *district* you should select in; *that* is a matter entirely for your own choice; but about the situation of your house I have a word or two to say. Very few selectors before coming here ever had the experience of choosing a site for a house or a farm homestead. In the old countries this is all done by landlord and builder; but so much of your future comfort, and also of your probable prosperity, depends upon this point that I intend to be explicit respecting it.

A point not to be lost sight of, more especially in a large holding, but also well worth taking into consideration by the holder of a small block, is, *to place the house and yards in as central a position* as possible. Even in a block of only 320 acres, if ever you come to cultivate and farm it properly, the saving of time in being in the middle of your paddocks is immense. You have not so far to cart your manure, and your cows do not take so long coming home. I was at one time of

E

my life a ploughman on a farm wh'ch was one mile long by half-a-mile broad, and the house was at one corner ; it was all arable ; many men were employed and several pairs of horses. The loss of time, not only by the men but also by the horses, coming and going, when we were cultivating the end fields, was then forcibly brought under my notice ; for we men took good care that the time expended in getting to and from work was not taken out of *our* time.

Now I have a grand caution to give you, which to the man of common sense may seem superfluous, but which the actual experience of colonial life shows to be constantly lost sight of or neglected. It is, do not be tempted under any circumstances whatever to *put up your house where there ever has been water over the ground;* no matter how long it is since the flood was, it will come again some day, and the longer it delays the more woe to you ; even if you are the least doubtful if the flood-level has been as high as the spot you would like to put your house on, *don't put it there!* do not let the nearness to the water tempt you. It certainly is very nice to only have to slip down the hill to the waterhole with a couple of buckets and bring it up as wanted ; but the day will come when you will rue it. Go farther up the rising ground and put your house there. An immense amount of misery and ruin would have been saved to hundreds of Australian settlers if these points had only been heeded. Mind, I do not say you are not to select a piece of low-lying land over which the flood-waters have been ; that is a matter for speculation on your part, for the very best of our lands are often such, and the flooding wonderfully adds to their fertility ; I only say do not on any account whatever *put your house on such.* In the one case you only lose a crop and some money, in the latter case you *may* lose house, wife, children, stock, and home. I speak strongly on this point, for I have seen many Australian floods. The creek is dry to-day, and has been dry for a year perhaps—looks as if no amount of rain could ever make it run again—to-morrow no dry land is to be seen ! Our floods are rapid in their rising, uncertain as to time, and destructive in their effects.

So much for danger from water ; now for another point of risk also very often neglected. Before you begin to put up your house, *cut down every native tree* that can by any possibility fall on to the house. Do not be tempted by the handsome appearance of any tree, or by the idea of shade from it in the summer time, to build under its area of reach in case it fell down. This danger may not seem of much importance to you as you gaze on a fine big gum-tree in calm weather, but in windy weather, on stormy nights, its removal will save your wife, if not yourself, from many a sleepless anxious night ! Our Australian trees, as a general rule, are not calculated to stand alone when they have been all their lifetime accustomed to the shelter of the surrounding forest ; so the more you clear your farm the more does the danger increase from any isolated tree near your house. Again, although a tree may not fall in a gale, our trees are so many of them **rotten at heart** that huge branches are constantly snapping off. I speak from experience on this subject as well as about the floods, for at one time I rented a farm on which my predecessor had put up the house, and there were several large trees left around it. Well, one day a gale came; I was working in the fields, but knowing how anxious my wife would be about those trees, I left off work and went home. Just as I got in sight of the house an extra blast of wind came, and I actually saw—the thought makes me shudder even now—the very tree I was most suspicious of (it was a gigantic gum) falling towards the house; it fell with a fearful crash, but, thank God! it was a little too short, and only the twigs and light top-branches touched the roof, but it broke to pieces the back door. Fortunately my wife had kept the children in, for if they had been (as they usually were) playing about the back yard, they would have been crushed. I know several similar cases; they are but too frequent; so—no matter what hurry you are in to put up your little house—*cut down the trees first*.

Another precaution I will also give you. If your land is in long-grassed country, then *burn or cut the grass* for some space around where you are going to put the house, or it *may* happen that a spark from your pipe, or a whirlwind among the ashes of your outside fire, may cause the grass to ignite, and, before you know it, all your slabs, shingles, or timber will be gone.

Choose a nice, dry, gravelly ridge, if you can get it, for the situation of the house and yards. Do not be tempted by the extra nearness of water to build on a mud or clay soil, if you can get a ridge or a sandhill; nearness to water is only of moment in the very first or incipient stage of selecting. As soon as you have got a horse and cart and can cart your water, it matters very little whether the waterhole is a quarter or half a mile off; the time and trouble is in the yoking up, the loading, and unloading, and not the actual distance the horse goes. The superior comfort to your wife, and through her to yourself, in a house built upon a nice dry ridge, over one built on a clay flat, is immense. Queensland clays are most tenacious, and stick to the boots in lumps as big as horses' heads; all this brought into a nice clean house is enough to spoil the temper of the most amiable woman. Of course I do not mean you to construe this advice into putting your house on such a rocky or barren spot that you cannot have a garden, for I believe in a garden around the house; but more about this directly.

TENT LIFE.

It may be that for some time you will have to live in a tent while your house is building and you are in a hurry to get your first crop in; especially is this likely to be the case if you have selected land in our interior, where timber is scarce and carriage of iron, etc., expensive. So a word or two on how to make your tent comfortable may, perhaps, be of use to some who very likely never lived in a tent before. Tents can be made very comfortable, and in our climate are quite sufficient protection from the weather if properly put up and lined. It is not the cold that is to be feared in a tent, but the extreme heat of a summer's day; the rain can be easily kept out, but on a hot day the interior of a tent is quite unbearable—hot as an oven—unless it is protected by a "fly" or false roof. This fly is an absolute necessity, not only for comfort but also for health; and if you have a wife and family whose work necessarily causes them to be much in the tent in the daytime, it is simply brutal not to put up a fly. It has many a time pained me sadly, when I have been travelling along a newly made section of railway, or at a "new rush," to see the poor women suffering the purgatory of these flyless tents.

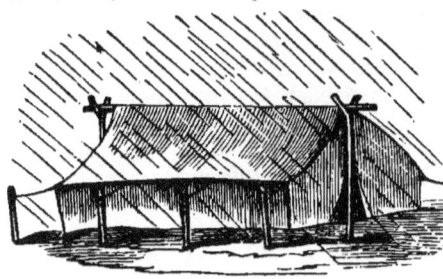

A TENT WITHOUT A FLY, AND IMPROPERLY PITCHED WITH STAKES, IN A SQUALL.

A tent badly pitched—that is, in the usual manner, according to the maker's idea, with pegs and stakes—is a great discomfort, for, tighten the ropes how you will, and make it nice and trim in fine weather, when the wet comes the cords shrink and pull any stake loose, for the ground at the same time gets sodden; then an extra blast of wind comes, and away goes everything; but a tent erected on a light frame of either round saplings or sawn battens is always strong and taut, and with a fly over is very comfortable. If you cannot get light sawn battens— 2 in. by 2 in. or 3 in. by 2 in. or 3 in. by 1 in.—then light round saplings will do; these you must bark, also take off all knots, or the calico will soon work into a hole; make the frame just big enough to go *altogether* inside the tent. For the "fly," put up at each end a stout fork well rammed into the ground and 1 foot taller than the tent. Across these place a second ridge pole; let this be stout and strong—it also must be barked and made smooth, or the constant flapping of the fly will quickly tear or wear it. Put the fly over the ridge and bring down the two ends; these are best fastened to a horizontal pole resting on two forks, exactly like a little ridge pole, placed 1 foot away from the sides of the tent; these poles need not be barked or smoothed, as only the cords of the fly are tied round them, but the forks must be very firmly put in the ground, for the fly has to stand the main strain of the wind.

Unbleached calico is quite stout enough for a tent in this climate, and, with a fly of the same material over, is quite water and weather-proof. Another great comfort in tent life is a bough shade put up in front of the tent; this is often done but far oftener not done,

FRAME TENT, WITH "FLY" COVERING.

and in the interest of suffering womankind in our hot climate I now mention it, so as to impress its necessity upon any new arrival or others who may read this. It is only a few hours' work; just cut six or eight strong forks, some 8 feet long; put these firmly in the ground 2 feet deep, lay other spars across these forks, and place gum, tea-tree, oak, or any boughs with leaves, upon them, and you have a rough but cool verandah under which the women-folk can wash, cook, and do all the work, and under which you can sit, work, and take your meals, and so keep the tent clean for sleeping in.

All tents should have a gutter or little ditch cut round them on the outside, so as to catch the water that drips off the fly and also the storm water that comes down from the higher ground. Do not put this simple matter off till the rain comes, or you will be disgusted to find your provisions and things saturated and your little house made damp and uncomfortable for days.

TENT, SHOWING ROUGH SHADE OF BOUGHS IN FRONT.

If your tent is situated on a ridge where you can get drainage, then excavate the floor to the depth of 18 inches or 2 feet; it is a plan not often adopted in Australia—why, I hardly know—but having lived in such a tent once, and found it a most comfortable arrangement, I strongly recommend it. One thing is necessary—to run a drain some 8 inches deep under the floor and out through the door, and so down the hill. If the land be level and this cannot be done, do not excavate at all, or you make a hole for the water to lodge in. After excavating, line with small stakes driven 6 inches into the ground and coming up just as high as the natural surface; this keeps the earth from falling into the tent every time the sides are touched. Now line the whole of the sides with blanketting, calico, osnaberg, or any old material, and your house will be very comfortable indeed. In a tent I lived in for many months, when on the Victorian diggings, the excavation was only in the middle; and the two sides, left the natural height of the surface, served my mate and myself as bunks to sleep on, and also as places for our boxes and things. Of course, we had a ditch on the outside as well as the inside drain, and the place was dry and cool. It was placed on the sides of one of the usual barren gravel ridges so common in gold districts. If you can get a few old packing cases to make a rough sort of floor all the better; it is a great addition to your comfort. If your land is in a heavily-timbered district you had better not go to the expense and bother of a tent at all, but put up a bark "humpy"—as we call it in Queensland—that is, make a frame as if for a tent, only taller, stronger, and bigger, and cover this frame with sheets of bark stripped from the trees. But if you go in for bark at all you may as well put up a "hut" at once.

As you are just from the old countries of Europe the idea of living in a bark house may seem strange, for such houses are, as far as my recollection goes, quite unknown there; but I can assure you that they are very comfortable, being warm in winter and cool in summer.

They are at best but ugly-looking things—it is impossible to put a finish on them—nevertheless, for a new selector, they are an admirable makeshift and will last for five or six years, or till you have funds enough to put up a permanent house.

It is a very great help to a selector to be located where he can get bark handy ; the barn, stables, pig-pen, calf-pen, and all outhouses can with it be easily and quickly made, and the frightful expense of buying iron and weatherboards, or the labour of, or time employed in, splitting shingles avoided. Being from a land where thatched houses are common, you may perhaps say : Why not use the long Queensland grass for a roof ? So I now take this opportunity to counsel you *never to*, if you can possibly avoid it, *put a thatched roof on* a house or even on an outhouse. This climate is very different to that of Europe : in our dry seasons the danger from bush fires is very great; scores of miles of country are burnt in a single day ; the whole land around you may be invisible from the smoke of the burning grass, shrubs, and trees ; these fires rage with fearful force and great rapidity, the sparks fly ahead for hundreds of yards, and a single one falling upon your thatched roof—which is now like tinder—will fire the whole homestead. If you are located in our far interior where there are no trees, then you must perforce use grass, but do not do so anywhere that you can possibly avoid it. This is no needless caution, for bush fires will be anxiety enough for your mind, without the extra anxiety that you may lose your home and all, as well.

METHOD OF CUTTING THE BARK BEFORE REMOVING THE SHEETS.

There are many of our trees off which you can strip large sound sheets of bark—namely, the blackbutt, stringybark, box, messmate, &c. As these will all be new to you—if you are going to select without any preliminary colonial experience—you must get some neighbour to point out the different sorts. He may also be able to show you how to go about stripping, but, in case he is not, I will give you just a few hints. The tools you will require are a sharp light axe, a tomahawk, a strong spade, and a light ladder made by nailing some strips of deal —old packing case will do—on two saplings about 10 feet long. Choose a straight, healthy-looking tree, of a size about 4 feet through ; with your axe cut through the bark, to the sapwood, a ring all round the tree about 3 feet from the ground ; then mount your ladder, and, with the tomahawk, cut a similar girdle 6 feet or 8 feet higher up, or the height that you wish your sheet to be long; next cut the bark through in a perpendicular line from the lower to the upper ring; a 3 feet wide sheet will be quite broad enough for you to experiment upon at first; so cut four of these upright lines—that is, divide the circumference of the tree into four parts—and you will get four sheets, each 3 feet by 8 feet out of the one girdle. You will find that you can cut through the fibres of our tough barks better by zig-zagging the cuts, like a herring-bone stitch, than by straight cuts. Now, with your axe start the edge of the bark the whole length of the upright cut; then insert your stout spade, the back of it next the bark, front next the wood; and by carefully working it you will find that—if the tree is in a fit state to strip at all—the bark will slip off easily. Use care so as not to make any cracks in the sheet, or you will spoil it for roofing purposes, although a sheet with a crack in does well enough for the walls of the house. If the tree is of less diameter than 4 feet you will find a considerable curve in the bark when taken off; do not put your foot upon it and crush it flat, or you will split it, but make a fire and put the sheet over it, inner side next the fire, and so steam it for a while; you will then be able to press it quite flat. Now take the spade and scrape off all the rough outside bark, until you have thinned the sheet considerably; put the four sheets one on the top of the other, and at once weight with two heavy logs, and leave till wanted.

If the bark does not slip off the tree easily, scrape the rough outside off with the spade, and then hammer the sheet well with a maul, without rings on, but with a handle long enough to let you reach to nearly the top of the cut. Trees strip best in spring, summer, or autumn; but there is no certainty about them, for the same kind of tree sometimes varies in different localities and according to whether it is a dry or a wet year. Off a tall tree you may get more than one length of bark, but you want a longer ladder; it also is awkward working so high up. If the tree is long enough to yield three or four lengths it is worth your while thinking whether it would not be better to cut the tree down and then strip it, for the tree may come in by-and-by for splitting into posts, rails, or slabs.

Having got a dozen sheets you can easily, by putting them up tent fashion against a ridge-pole, make temporary but weather-proof accommodation for yourself and things while you are erecting the hut.

BARK HUTS.

May be some of the readers of this will think it folly to dwell upon such an erection as a "bark" hut, but there are advantages connected with this simple kind of dwelling which greatly commend it to a new selector, and especially to a new-comer who has not yet

TEMPORARY BARK "HUMPY."

had any experience in bush handicraft. Even if you are a man who has no skill in the use of carpenters' tools you may venture to put up a bark hut, when, if you tried your hand at a slab hut, you would most surely get "bogged;" for a bark hut requires no adzing, squaring, splitting, or morticing, yet can be made strong and comfortable; it is, moreover, speedily erected, and, as I said above, is warm in winter, cool in summer, and thoroughly rain-proof. All the tools you require are a cross-cut saw (6 feet long is a handy size for general selection work), hand-saw, hammer, gimlet, and the tools you used when getting the bark; also procure several pounds weight of wire nails 3 inches to 6 inches long. Supposing you to be a married man, you cannot well be comfortable with less than four rooms, including kitchen; you may do with less, but you will sacrifice decency and comfort, and my object in these papers is to show you how to be comfortable—for a successful man is not necessarily a rich man, but one who has all the comforts he desires.

A hut 24 feet by 12 feet, and walls 8 feet high, divided into two rooms, and with a "lean-to" behind, 9 feet wide, of two rooms, one of which is the kitchen, will do very well, especially with a verandah in the front. All the timber you require for this can be round spars and saplings as got in the bush; they will need no trimming, except to take off the bark and branches; even if they are not particularly straight they will do, for, with bark, exactness is not looked for or necessary. Let your corner posts be 8 inches thick (big end) by 10 feet long; saw the top off level and put the posts 2 feet deep in the ground. Begin by putting the two front ones in at each corner—that is 24 feet apart; and before finally fixing stretch a cord across the top from one to the other. Now stand off some twenty yards and see if it is level; if not, raise or lower the posts till it is; see that the posts are upright, and then ram the earth all round them till they are quite firm. Next put one in the centre, the same size and depth in the ground, then put between these other posts—less stout will do, and not so deep in the ground—every 4 feet. Keep the line stretched tight along the top, and saw off level to it. Now get a straight spar 24 feet 6 inches long, about 6 inches through at the thick end, and lay it on the posts; let someone hold it while you mark on it each side of every post where they touch. Take down this wall-plate again and saw nicks, where the marks are, half-way through the plate. If you cannot use an adze you can now cut out the slots with a tomahawk. Replace the plate, and nail on to each post with a 6-inch wire nail, and you have the front frame of your house up. Proceed exactly the same with the back frame; be careful that it is parallel and square with the one already up. Next put a wall-plate across each and one across the middle; halve them into the front and back wall-plates, and nail firmly as well. Put a post in the middle of these ends and centre division wall, 2 feet deep in the ground, but let it be 13 feet out, or as high as you intend the ridge-pole to be. Where this touches the wall-plate, halve it into it—that is, take a piece, half way through, out of both post and wall-plate and nail together. Do the same with the other end and with the middle division; put a light spar along the top of these three uprights, and nail on as you did the wall-plates; this is for a ridge-pole. Put other uprights every 4 feet apart in the end walls and division, and nail on. Now get some light spars, some 3-inch or 4-inch thick, and as long as to reach from wall-plate to ridge-pole—that will be about 8 feet long; cut a little out where

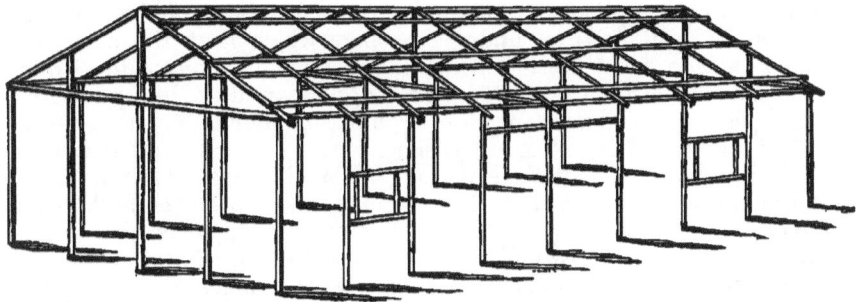

FRAMEWORK FOR TWO-ROOMED BARK HUT.

they touch, and nail on. Put one every 3 feet on each side of the ridge; these are your rafters. This roof will want staying, else a heavy gale of wind coming on to either end would cause it to yield lengthways; so get two spars long enough to reach from the end of the ridge-pole to the centre of the division wall-plate; nail in that position; do the same with the opposite end. Now nail three light spars across the rafters—one near the top, one in the middle, and one near the bottom; these are to hold the bark up. Nail similar battens all round the upright walls, except, of course, where you are going to have the windows and doors. All the posts being in the ground, there

BARK HUT, WITH VERANDAH AND LEAN-TO BEHIND.

ought to be no occasion for diagonal stays to them; but if you think it needs them, then put some. The frame is now complete and ready for the bark; so get a sheet, scrape off the rough outside, and put it on the roof. Try and get the sheets long enough to reach from ridge to wall-plate; it makes a much neater job where there is no joining in the roof, and is better too, for the bark can be pressed flatter. Give each sheet 1 foot overlap of its next neighbour on the roof; for the wall a lap of only a few inches will be sufficient. Over the ridge place the sheets lengthways, bending the sides down; but take great care you do not split them, for a split in the ridge will let in the wet sooner than any other place. Make a hole in the top end of each sheet that goes on the roof, fasten a strip of green hide or fencing wire to it, and as each sheet is handed up tie it to the top batten; this is not to hold the bark down, but just to stop it slipping from under the spars which keep the bark flat, hinder the sun from curling it up, or the wind blowing it off. To fix the spars on wire is the best - the old plan used to be by hanging spars pegged to the horizontal ones; but you should buy a hundred-weight or two of No. 8 good fencing-wire—you will find it always coming in useful for all sorts of things. Well, get a spar the length of the house and about 6 inches through, lay it upon the bark about 3 feet from the top, lay a similar spar on the opposite side of the ridge, and tie these two together, every 6 feet or so, by strands of wire; the wire being pliable will bend over the ridge, and so keep the sheet of bark that does duty for a ridge-cap always nicely curved. Now place another pair of similar spars about 1 foot from the eaves and suspend from the ones above, and your roof is fixed and firm; it will keep out wind and rain, heat and cold.

The sheets are best fixed on to the upright walls by placing, outside of the bark, light spars as battens exactly on a line with the battens on the inside, and binding these two together by means of wire, making a gimlet-hole for the wire to go through the bark; if the bark is thin you may nail the two battens together instead, and it makes a much neater job. For the two back rooms and the front verandah proceed in exactly the same way as you have done for the main building, but be sure that the roof-sheets of the "lean-to" go well under the upper ones. Six feet will be quite high enough for the uprights of the back wall, and the best plan of fixing the rafters is to nail the top end on to the corresponding rafter of the main building, about a foot and a-half from its end; this gives you considerably more slope for the roof of these back rooms.

FIREPLACES AND CHIMNEYS FOR BUSH HUTS.—Any new-comer will, after reading my previous remarks on bark huts, find no difficulty in erecting one; but I said nothing about a fireplace or chimney, and much comfort, not only to the wife but also to the master of the house, depends upon having a comfortable fireplace—one that will be large enough to allow a big fire to be made in it; one that will not make the wife cross, or injure her eyes by continually smoking, nor catch fire, and so burn down the hut some day when you are absent; one that will hold a large log, and so save the trouble of cutting the wood into small pieces (which is one of the greatest nuisances in the bush, and which, I am sorry to say, is too often left for the woman to do). While living in a tent you can do your cooking under a rough shelter made by placing forked uprights in the ground at the four corners of a 6-feet square—the two front ones about 6 feet high out of the ground, the two back ones about 5 feet; across these lay two spars and one or two light battens, and cover with a couple of sheets of bark; around the back and two sides build a wall of loose stones or sods to about half-way up, and that is all that is required. Put a bough shade in front of this, and you have a very comfortable kitchen for fine or hot weather; in fact, you will find, if you put up a table under this shade, that you will prefer, during the hot weather, taking your meals under it to being under cover of a tent. It is astonishing how an expert bush cook will get through work with no better cooking-place than such a one as I have just described. I have known *one* man cook for fifty shearers, and cook well, too—for shearers are most exacting upon their cooks—with nothing but this bark "kitchen." The utensils you will require for such a place are a camp-oven, iron pot, bucket, tin "billy," fryingpan, tin plates and dishes, sheath knives, iron forks and spoons, pannikins, and an old spade. With this simple and cheap assortment your wife will, when she gets used to the camp-oven management and the colonial method of using hot ashes, turn out such a dinner as would, in the old country, be the envy of the parish.

But if you have a hut—even if it is only a bark one—I advise you to have the fireplace attached to it. Although Queensland is hot enough and to spare in summer, yet our winter months are biting cold; we do not have any snow and but seldom a strong frost, still the cold in this climate penetrates a person who has resided here a summer more than it does in England, and a fire in winter is very welcome indeed. Also, it is more comfortable for your wife to have the kitchen indoors, especially in case of sickness—and all through these pages you will find me *earnestly advocating the woman's comfort;* it is far too often overlooked by our new settlers. Leave a 5-feet wide gap in the back wall of one of the back rooms of the hut; this is not a bit too wide for a good bush fireplace, and we will have it 5 feet deep also— that is, a square of 5 feet. At the two outside corners erect upright tapering spars 6 inches thick at the butt end, and let these be a *little higher out of the ground than the ridge of the roof;* put them 2 feet deep in the ground; put also a similar spar between each of these and the house, but let it be only 18 inches from the corner upright. These four will form the shaft of the chimney, and it will be 5 feet by 18 inches in size. See that these are all quite upright, then join all together by several crosspieces nailed on to the outsides; also join to the house by a crosspiece near the ground, and one 5 feet up as well; do the same on the other side. Now get a sheet of thin (not cor-rugated) iron, 6 feet long and 2 feet 6 inches wide; double this length-ways into a V shape, but let the one leg of the V be 2 feet wide and the other 6 inches. Nail the short flap—keeping the bent side down— to the outside of the wall of the house, over the gap left for the fire-place, and the height up that you want the mantelshelf to be—that is, about 5 feet from the floor. Nail one end of a light spar to the upright of the hut just under this sheet of iron, and take the other end to the outside one of the chimney spars, letting it touch it at about 4 feet from the top; halve it into both uprights, and nail; do the same to the opposite side. These act as stays to the shaft, and also contract the opening. Now fasten down the long or 2 feet flap of the sheet of iron to these two stays, and you have a gutter formed between the chimney and the house which *will never let in the rain* however much it pours down. You can now nail or fasten on the bark, placing battens across according to the size of the sheets, just as you did for the hut. Let the sheets covering the sloping or roof part of the chimney come well over the edge of the sheet of iron. It would be better to place another sheet of iron, or some old sheets of tin cases, underneath these sloping sheets of bark; it would then not matter how big a blaze there chanced to be in the fire, for there are *no beams or anything overhead* which could catch fire. The usual way of building a bush chimney is to contract the shaft from all sides but the back to a diameter of from 1 foot to 2 feet, but this would be far more difficult for you—whom I am supposing to have as yet but little skill with tools—to do. Also the cross-beams necessary frequently get on fire after they become old and dry; and, besides, my experience is that these contracted narrow-necked chimneys *often smoke*, whereas the simply-built one I advocate will not. A little rain may come down my wide flue, but as it all falls at the very back of the fireplace, it does no harm. I am writing this before a fine fire made in a fireplace like this, and, although 18 inches rain fell in two days of last week, we never had any trouble with the fire. You will have to line the inside of the fireplace with sheets of old tin or iron, to the height of 4 feet, or, if you cannot get this, then you must build a rough wall of stones and mortar all round the inside. You have only one thing more to do to make sure that your chimney will not smoke—that is, *raise the floor of the fireplace* to quite 1 foot higher than the floor of the hut. This is a wrinkle not generally known. It alone will often, but not always, cure the smoking of bush fireplaces, even with the most contracted of chimneys. But with a straight flue such as I have just described, a raised floor, the chimney shaft as high as the ridge, and no cracks in it, you *will never be troubled with smoke*, no matter how hard or what direction the wind blows.

TREE-FALLING AND TOOLS.

I spoke previously of bark huts; you may very likely, however, be able to afford the expense and time of erecting a substantial *slab hut* at once, but, before you can do this, it is necessary you should know something of tree-falling and the tools you will want. Nothing but practical experience will teach you this properly, and if you can afford to hire a good bush carpenter *it is your best and quickest mode of learning*; but in order that you may not be completely under his "tyranny" (for the old hands know well how to "come the boss" over a new-comer) I will give you a few hints; very likely, too, you may not be able to afford to pay for labour, but prefer building your hut yourself, room by room, as you get the opportunity.

The tools you will want are—an *American axe*, not too heavy—as you are not used to an axe, rather err on the side of lightness; a *cross-cut saw* 6 feet long. One of the most useful tools you can buy is the "*one-man American cross-cut saw*"—it is about 4 feet 6 inches long, and, as the name implies, can be worked by one man; I can vouch from my own experience for its being the most handy and useful saw for any selector. As I do not suppose you will at first be inclined to tackle a very big tree, this one-man tool will do instead of the 6 feet double cross-cut, but see that it has a loop at the end for fixing another handle; it can then be worked by two men if required, and will serve for trees not more than 3 feet through. Directions for sharpening these American saws are printed on the saw itself; read these carefully, and copy them out before they get rusted off. Buy several files suitable to the saw, and also a common saw-set. A thoughtful man, after reading these plain directions, will find no great difficulty in sharpening his saw; it only wants care and thought. This saw-sharpening is one of the things which out in these colonies you, the master farmer, *must* learn to do; if you do not—as you cannot get the tool into town to get done every time it wants it, and as many of the old bush hands who say they can sharpen a saw know nothing of the principle of it, but will spoil your nice thin Yankee blade the first time they try— your arms will be almost pulled off dragging the blunt unset tool backwards and forwards, and yet do no good; so my advice is, learn to sharpen and set it yourself, and *never* let any of your men do it. You must also buy a *grindstone;* it is a thing you cannot do without; however short of cash you may be, it is no good going into the bush without one. If you have money buy a set of anti-friction rollers and an iron axle and handle; they make the work much easier; but a good makeshift can be made with a bent wooden axle, obtained from some curved branch of a tree. Having got the stone, erect it the very first job, and always keep your axe sharp by giving it a light touch every morning before you go to work; it will then never want much grinding, unless you are so careless as to chip a gap in it by striking against the wedges when splitting a log; if you do you must grind the gap out before you can again use it with proper effect. Do not grind the edge only or you will make the axe too stunted, but grind a little off the checks every time as well; aim to preserve the fine gradual wedge shape it had when you bought it.

You will also want a *set of wedges*—six will do—some small and thin for entering—that is, beginning to split the log—and some longer and stouter; the largest may be 10 inches long by $2\frac{1}{2}$ inches broad, and 2 inches thick at the head; do not have the bottom edge hammered too thin by the smith, but use the grindstone to it instead; by this method they are not so apt to turn or twist when they come against a knot. Before beginning work you will want a "*maul,*" as it is called in the colonies—"beetle" I have heard it called in England; that is, get a piece of hard tough wood, 9 inches long and 6 inches through, pare the two ends down to a thickness of 5 inches, or whatever size your maul-rings are—a handy size for these is 5 inches diameter, $1\frac{1}{4}$

inch broad, and ⅓ inch thick; but every man hash is own fancy about the size and weight of a maul. Slip these tightly one over each end, and let the wood project ¾ inch. Now bore a 1-inch hole perfectly true through the centre between the two rings, and insert a round, smooth, tough handle, about 2 feet 8 inches or 2 feet 10 inches long; drive a wedge into the end that goes through the maul, and if properly done it will not come off even with the excessive hammering it will have to do. But I am telling you to bore a hole, and yet have not told you what to do it with; you must buy three augers—¾-inch, 1-inch, and 1½-inch (you will want all these when building your hut); get the sort called "*shell*" augers, for as sure as ever you, unaccustomed to boring, begin to work with the ordinary bush auger you will snap off the worm screw and the thing is then useless; besides, the shell sort never choke up (I have never tried them in very hard dry wood), and one of the commonest and most irritating nuisances to the bush worker is this choking of augers. I always use "Gilpin's patent"; these, if kept quite clean and sharp, work well, but not otherwise. To start the hole for a shell auger, take out half an inch or so with a gouge or round chisel.

I now suppose you are anxious to set to work to knock down your maiden tree. The love of destruction being so inherent in mankind, you will find that you will always experience a pleasure—as if of overcoming a difficulty—of conscious power, when you see a gigantic gumtree falling, the result of the repeated strokes of your own sharp axe. Do not stand, and look, and think how big the tree is, and that you can never get it down, and that you had better look for a smaller one; if it is straight, and therefore likely to split easily, then set to work at it; it will soon come down, and the bigger it is the more slabs or posts you will get.

To cut down a tree seems a very simple thing to do, and no newcomer would admit that he could not do it. I have several times taken a freshly-arrived immigrant at his word and set him to work at a tree, and it is invariably the case that, although he will get the tree down it is with a greater expenditure of strength than is necessary, and also with considerable danger to himself.

The accompanying sketch will show you better than any description how to go about it. However, I will explain it somewhat. Do not chop all round the tree till you get it standing like a peg-top on its point; that is what all new-comers (if they have never done any wood-cutting before—as few have) invariably do, and therein lies the danger to themselves, for if the tree is upright, without any decided lean, it is impossible to say which way it will fall; a puff of wind, or an extra preponderance of branches on one side, may slew it quite round upon the top of you. Choose the tree you want; notice which side it leans to; then, on the *underneath* or *leaning side*, proceed to chop out a gap, as shown in the picture; keep the bottom of the chop level, by using the axe horizontally or across the cut, but make the cut with a slope by using the axe from above downwards; when this is properly carried out the butt of the fallen tree will be wedge-shaped, but the top of the stump will be almost as level as if sawn across ; not that it matters as far as appearance goes, whether the old stump is level or uneven, but by making it level there is, when you get used to the work, no unnecessary chopping. The main thing to tell you about this is, to *make the chop or gap wide enough*, so as to give plenty of room for your axe to work when you are getting near the middle of the tree; for which reason the thicker the tree the wider must this chop be. Nothing is more common than to see a new hand, who thinks he is saving himself trouble by only taking out a narrow chop, get hopelessly " bogged " and distressed, as, finding his axe will not bite, he uses more and more unnecessary strength, the only result being a blunting of the axe, and maledictions uttered against the Australian trees.

Having cut the tree half or nearly half-way through, next proceed to the other or upper side ; do the same there, and, when you get sufficiently far through, the tree will fall harmlessly over in the direction of the first cut, and away from yourself. When the tree begins to crack and show signs of falling *do not be so foolish as to run away;* for if it *should* happen to fall the way you ran the top branches would most assuredly catch you before you could get out of their reach, and you would be killed; but stand by the trunk, a few feet away, coolly watch which way it is going over, then quietly walk a few more feet away from it.

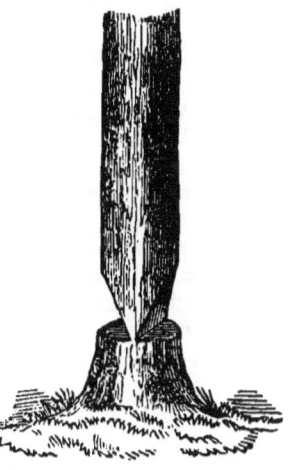

THE PROPER WAY TO CUT THE TREE WHEN FALLING IT WITH AN AXE.

It may be that you have got a tree so upright that you cannot judge which way it will fall; in such case, if there is any wind blowing, treat the lee side as the leaning side. You will now see that by cutting the chop on the butt of the tree wedge or ▷ shaped, it can only fall *two* ways, whereas if you cut it peg-top fashion it may *twist round on itself and fall any way;* so do not be tempted, when the bottom of the tree is assuming the shape of a thin wedge, to chop in from the side, thinking that you can thereby hasten its falling. If the tree is large, but short in the barrel, and has a top of heavy strong branches, these branches may, by touching the ground first on falling, cause the butt to " kick up," and perhaps fall down again alongside the stump, exactly where you were standing when you gave the last chop; therefore do not remain close to the stump when once you *see for certain* that the tree is going. There is another cause of kicking, the result of careless cutting of the under-cut, that is far more dangerous ; I will try and point it out to you. If the tree is leaning over considerably, then it is somewhat difficult to work the underneath cut, and you, perhaps, think " Oh, it is certain to fall that way," so you start on the upper side without bothering with an under-cut. Well, when you have got half-way through, the tree falls, the *trunk split's up* for many feet, the butt is hoisted high in the air, and, through using the uncut half as a fulcrum or purchase, is actually forced backwards a considerable distance behind the stump as it falls to the ground. This is more likely to occur when you use a cross-cut saw to fall with, instead of an axe, for the saw gets pinched by the pressure of the leaning tree before you have got the cut far enough towards the centre; in such a case even upright trees will split up and so be useless as timber, beside being dangerous to the faller. If you prefer to use the cross-cut saw, do so only on the upper side, using the axe for the under or leaning side, until you have gained some experience in wood-craft. Before commencing work cast a look up to the top and notice whether any of the branches are inlocked with a neighbouring tree, or are rotten, and so likely to break off and fall where you are standing as the tree goes over; it is astonishing what a severe hit even only a small branch will give when it falls from a good height.

If the tree in falling catches in another, and remains so suspended, *do not bother any more with it,* for to cut the tree down that supports it requires a man far more experienced in axe-work than you will be for some time. It is always a dangerous operation; better sacrifice the time you have spent upon it than risk your life *for the sake of a few slabs.*

To teach axe-craft by writing only is impossible, but the above hints may help you somewhat; however, set boldly to work and you will soon find out a "thousand and one" little wrinkles which cannot be written about. The best practical advice I can give you is: If you can afford it, hire a good old-fashioned "bush-carpenter" for a few weeks; you will then see how things are done.

SPLITTING SHINGLES.

Being fresh from a land where slates, tiles, and thatch are the principal materials used for roofing purposes, it is very likely you do not even know what a "shingle" is. Well, then, look up at the older houses in Brisbane, and you will see that they are roofed with narrow strips of wood, laid, slate fashion, one over the other. That is a "shingle" roof, and, as it is an exceedingly comfortable and durable one, I purpose now giving you some directions upon the method of splitting them, so that you can roof your slab house with something more sightly than bark. Another reason I have is, that if you are located anywhere near a new township, you may there get a considerable sale for shingles; even if you have not the timber on your own selection you can, by paying a fee of £2 a year to the nearest clerk of petty sessions, get a license to go on any Crown lands and cut what timber you want, not only for your own use but also for sale; if you cut pine or soft wood, then the license-fee is £4. Very likely the "bush carpenter" you may have hired to help you with the hut may know nothing about splitting shingles, for since the introduction of galvanised iron they are not so much in demand as they were in the early days. Still, for a bush house, in which the roof is necessarily low down, as compared with town houses, shingles are by far the best (because cooler) roof for our hot climate. They have the disadvantage of requiring more rafters than iron or bark, for they are a great weight, and also they require a large number of sawn battens or light spars, adzed quite smooth or level, on which they rest and are nailed.

The best shingles are the *narrowest*; from 2¾ inches to 4½ inches is, in my experience, the best width. I have seen them 6 inches wide, and these stand the weather well, but more often these wide ones will *crack* or curl up; so do not go beyond the 4½ inch, for there is no occasion for you to run the risk of a leaky roof. In length make them 15 inches or 18 inches, and the thickness ⅜ inch to ½ inch. Do not strive how thin you can split them, if you have got hold of a very easy splitting tree; the thick ones are the best for they do not crack. One thing is absolutely necessary: *they must be straight and flat* —no curve or twist of any sort in them. For splitting slabs or shingles, posts or rails, it is essential that you should choose a tree that *will* split. To tell you by writing what tree will split is impossible; it is an art only learned by experience, but a few hints may help you in acquiring that experience. Fix on a tree whose bark runs in a grain quite straight up and down, for as is the grain of the bark so runs the grain of the wood, although it is not always the case that a tree with straight running bark will split. To help you further, knock off some bark and chip out a piece of the wood from the butt, some 8 inches square and to a depth of some 3 inches, and notice whether it is "free"—that is, if it parts easily; but the degree of freeness necessary you can only learn to judge of by trial. If the bark is curly— that is, if the grain runs in waves from side to side—you can knock the tree down if you like and try it, but you will never again knock a curly one down, for you will have found out that the wood is just as curly as the bark, and each fibre tightly inlocked with its neighbour, and so quite impossible to split. Any of our hardwoods that will split will do well for shingles, provided they are not made too thin.*

The bigger the tree the better for shingle-splitting, so choose one not less than 4 feet through; if it is "pipey"—that is hollow all up the centre—it does not matter; it is just as good, if not better, than the sound tree, for you must not make use of the very heart.

After the tree has fallen, knock off the bark, saw off the wedge-shaped butt-end and then

Fig. 1—FALLEN TREE, SHOWING HOW TO CUT INTO SECTIONS FOR SHINGLES.

saw the rest of the log up into cuts exactly the breadth you intend the shingles to be *long* (fig. 1). Now turn one of these sections face up on the ground, and with a carpenter's pencil mark it as I am about to

---

* The best wood for shingles is spotted-gum, as it does not colour the water.—ED.

F

tell you. We will suppose the tree is 4 feet across; then all around the edge mark off every 4½ inches—the width you do not intend the shingles to exceed. A very good rough guide for these 4½-inch marks is the breadth of your hand as laid flat on the edge of the block. Having marked all round (in a tree 4 feet through there will be thirty-two of these marks), take a straight-edged bit of deal and draw a line from any one of these outside marks (see A fig. 2) to the centre of the stump; now draw a similar line from the adjoining mark (C) again to the centre. As you do not want the shingles to be a less width than 2¾ inches, have a piece of wood just that length, and with it measure and mark where the lines are *exactly that width apart*; it will be about D. Next, with a pencil fastened to a bit of string and the other end of the string fastened to a nail driven into the centre of the block, draw the circle D, E, F, D, and mark it off into 2¾-inch spaces, just as you did

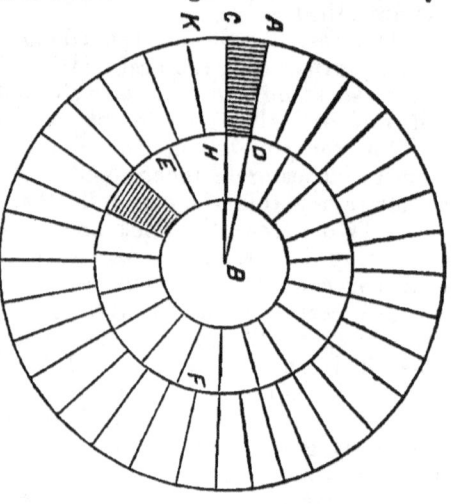

FIG. 2.—A BLOCK 4 FEET ACROSS MARKED FOR SPLITTING INTO "BILLETS."

the outside rim into 4½ inches; then draw lines from every outside mark to its corresponding inside one, as shown at K H, and you have all your "billets" nicely and exactly marked. All this may sound rather puzzling, but try it on the stump and it will in reality be found quite simple; once mastered you will find it very easy, and by it you will avoid any waste wood or irregular shingles, and you *cannot possibly make them either too broad or too narrow*. If the heart of the tree is sound you can get an inner layer of billets by treating the inner circle, D, E, F, D exactly the same as

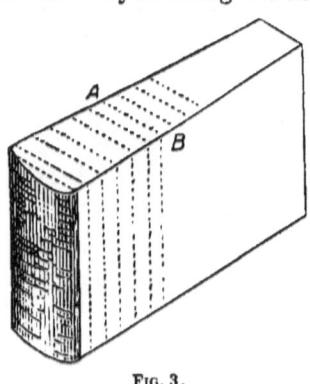

FIG. 3.

you did the outer one, but there is bound to be a centre piece of the very heart which it will be useless to split up. If the tree is "pipey" you can find the centre point and draw the circle all the same, by placing across the pipe a piece of old deal case. Now with your wedges and maul split this block in half, then into half again —that is into quarters—and again into half-quarters, but always keeping on to one of the lines. Now split off the inner circle of billets; you can then divide the outside into the divisions as marked, and you have the whole cut of the tree split up into pieces the shape of fig. 3, and ready to be further split into shingles. Each billet will be 18 inches tall by 4½ inches broad at the one end, and 2¾ inches at the thin end, and about 1 foot long, and will yield you, if the wood is all good, 24 shingles, or 768 in all, not counting the inner circle of billets, which should yield about 240, or 1,000 in the one cut of the tree. The quickest and handiest method of splitting these billets into shingles is this: Get a

FIG. 4.

fork of a tree 6 feet or 7 feet long, and the thickness of your thigh; place this flat across the stump of the fallen tree, the two prongs projecting 1 foot or so over to the right of the stump, and the butt end projecting a similar distance over the left, as you look at it. Notice that it rests firmly and is solid; lift up one of the "billets" and put it, end upwards, between the forks (as shown in fig. 4); the business of the fork is simply to hold the billet steady and keep the split pieces from falling on the stump. Now take your shingling "froe" (fig. 5)—a tool you must buy and can get at any bush store—in your left hand, and your mallet (fig. 6) in your right, lay the "froe" on the centre of the billet in the line A B (fig. 3), give it a smart hit with the mallet, and the billet falls in two. Divide the halves again, and again, and again, but always in the same direction as the first cut (see dotted lines, fig. 3) till each bit will just split into two shingles; a good gauge of the proper thickness of these is the breadth of the back edge of the "froe"; do *not* knock each shingle off by itself, but *halve, and halve each half*, as stated above.

FIG. 5.

By proceeding in this simple yet systematic manner you will waste but little wood, have but few inferior shingles, and the work will be a pleasure to you, except the sawing part, which is always laborious. If the tree does not split easily, leave it and fall another; and before you go to the bother of sawing off all the breadths try one and see how it will split.

The mallet (fig. 6) is simply a piece of tough knotty branch of a

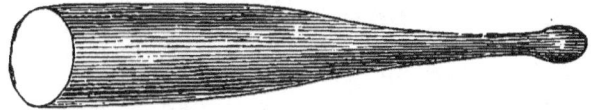

FIG. 6.

tree, about 4 inches thick and about 1 foot long; pare down one end till it is thin enough for your hand to grasp, and you use it as you would a club if you were going to knock down an enemy. Always, when not using the mallet, lay it down on the forks *to your right*, and lay the "froe" down on the *left*; they are thus always to hand.

SLAB HUTS.

In the early days of settlement in America the *log* cabin was almost the universal dwelling; in these colonies the slab hut takes its place; it is *the* hut of the bush, the "home" of the Australian settler, whether he be a rich squatter or a poor selector; and it is equally applicable to both, for on it can be spent hundreds of pounds if you want to be grand, or it can be put up for *less than a score*, if you are pinched for money or time. If *well* put up it will last you for many years, but if "slummed" it will soon get shaky and lean askew; for, having no diagonal stays, nothing but the wall-plates and tie-beams to hold it together (as the slabs themselves, not being nailed, but quite loose, give no additional stiffness), unless the corner posts are put deep in the ground it is the weakest of structures.

If you have mastered the details of shingle-splitting, you will find splitting the slabs for the hut comparatively easy, as the principle of the matter is the same, the only difference being the size; a shingle seldom measuring more than 18 inches in length, while a slab may be 6 feet, 7 feet, or 8 feet long, by any width you can knock out—the wider the better.

Before cutting down a tree you may perhaps be anxious to know how tall it is. In simple short work, like slab-splitting, you can guess pretty well how many lengths you can get out of a trunk, but as at some time or other of your bush life you may perhaps be able to obtain a contract to get telegraph poles, long beams, or piles for bridge-building, I will give you an easy plan by which you can tell the height of any tree whose shadow you can measure; it is more often only the height to the first fork or branch that you will require. Set up a stick 6 feet long, and when its shadow is equal to it—that is, when it is 6 feet—measure the length of the shadow of the tree, and *that will be the tree's height*. Or, if you do not choose to wait till the shadow is equal to the height of the stick, you can find it any time by a rule of simple proportion; thus, if a stick 6 feet tall throws a shadow 4 feet long, and a neighbouring tree throws a shadow 40 feet to the first fork, then the height to that fork will be 60 feet.

The longer the slabs the more "free" you require the tree to be: what I mean is, that you can knock 3 feet and 4 feet slabs out of almost any tree which is not decidedly curly, but for slabs 7 feet or 8 feet long you must pick the best splitting tree your judgment tells you of. Having felled the tree, mark off the lengths you want—whether 4 feet, 5 feet, 6 feet, or 8 feet—and, before beginning to saw, cut a rim of bark off from the track the saw will take, for the bark hinders it from working freely.

If the tree has fallen so that it rests upon its butt and one of its branches, and so has no support in the middle of the trunk, and you begin to saw off the cut, you will find that before you have got half-way through the saw will be so pinched by the log closing up that you will be unable to move it one way or the other, and you will even be puzzled how to get it out again. What you must do to avoid this is, before commencing the cut, to prop up the centre with a stout chock

FIG. 7.

of wood, so as to take the weight off one end, and, as the saw gets buried, drive in a wedge over it on the top of the cut. The drawing (fig. 7) will show you what I mean.

The next thing to do after sawing off the block is to "open it up"—that is, to split it into two equal halves; to do this, start the crack at one end (the top end is the best) by inserting two or three of

FIG. 8.

the smallest wedges, driving them in equally and a little at a time, and, as the crack opens, drive in the other and larger wedges along the top (see drawing, fig 8). In addition to the iron wedges you want two or three large wooden ones, which you can shape for yourself out of a piece of hardwood; make them 18 inches or 2 feet long and some 5 inches or 6 inches

thick at the butt. After starting the crack with the iron wedges, doubling them where required—that is, driving a fresh one in alongside one that is already driven "home"—insert the big wooden ones, drive them "home," and the log will fall in two. Some logs will want rolling over and working from the opposite side as well, and some will even require bursting open with gunpowder, but I cannot explain everything in these pages; I must of necessity leave much for you to learn by experience, and you must accept my writings and drawings only as so many "hints." Split the two halves again, making quarters, and, if the tree is a big one, again, making eighths. These pieces you must now split just the same as you did the shingles. I don't mean that you are to put them up on end as you did the billets out of which you knocked the shingles, but that the direction in which the slabs are to be run out is just the same as in the case of

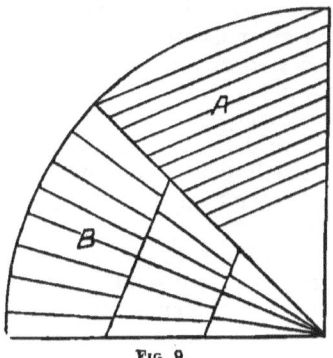

FIG. 9.

the shingles (see A, drawing, fig. 9). This is also the way to run off posts for your fencing, but in splitting rails for fencing you just go on dividing the eighths into sixteenths, and so on till you have them the size you require, or, if it is a big tree, then subdivide as you see done in the drawing (B, fig. 9).

All timber for building purposes will last much longer if felled in the winter time; the very worst time is in the spring, when the sap is in full vigour; but in our, at times, dry climate the full rush of the sap cannot be told to a month—it depends so much on whether rain has fallen or no.

I will suppose the size of your hut to be 24 feet by 12 feet; put up this well, and you can at any odd time add a "lean-to" behind, or at the sides, as you may fancy or require. The height of the rooms we will make 8 feet. The slabs can be put either upright or on their ends—that is, perpendicular, or lying down on their edges—that is, horizontal. I must confess to being strongly prejudiced in favour of the horizontal method, for it has several advantages: first, shorter slabs are required (a very great consideration if timber is scarce and hard to split); secondly, you can make the walls of the hut any height you like; thirdly, it is always weatherproof, for, as the slabs shrink, so they fall down by their own weight and leave no gaps between, whereas upright slabs, after being erected a few months, will have so shrunk that you can put your hand between any of them; also the horizontal slabs look much nicer; they certainly take a little longer to put up, but, as erecting dwelling-houses is not a thing you will be often doing, a little extra time spent to make your home look neater will not be time wasted. As this hut is to take the place of the bark one you first put up, of course you must intend to put a floor to it, so we will arrange for it to be 1 foot higher than the ground, but 18 inches or 2 feet would be better still—if you have no trouble to get straight posts long enough.

By the time you have felled the trees and split the slabs and shingles for the hut you will have become tolerably skilful in the use of the axe, saw, and wedges; but you will now have to try your hand at adze-work, for the adze is the principal tool required in erecting a slab house. It is a nasty tool for anyone not used to it to tackle, and you must use it with great care at first, keeping your legs out of the direction of the way you are cutting, or the result will be that you will get a most frightful cut on the foot or leg. As it is a tool *necessary for all bush work* you must not *shirk learning to use it*, awkward though you will find it; never mind, persevere, and by-and-by you will gain confidence, and perhaps be trying to emulate the ship carpenter by splitting a penny in two when held to the floor by the naked toe.

Get six round posts 12 feet long and not less than 12 inches through at the small end; these are for the corner and middle posts. Also get fifteen ditto, not so thick (6 inches will do), and 8 feet 8 inches long; also seven ditto, 12 feet long and 9 inches thick, for ground-plates; also two wall-plates, 24 feet by 6 inches thick, and three ditto, 12 feet by 6 inches, for end and middle wall-plates. You will now have to take your first lesson in squaring these logs; but, as this will be a trouble to you, I will not tell you to square anything that is not absolutely necessary. Begin with the ground-plate; knock off the bark, stretch a chalked line along its whole length, on both its sides and about one-third of its thickness down; a bit of charcoal rubbed on the line will do as well as chalk, and will leave a good black mark on the white surface of the fresh-barked saplings. It is a great difficulty with new bushmen to get these two chalked lines on the same level, and the consequence is that, when intending to make a square post, it comes out with four flat sides certainly, but the post itself is *lozenge* shaped. I will try and show you how to do it. Look at the drawing, fig 10. A B is the chalked line; before striking it, saw off both ends of the log *quite straight across* the log—that is, at *exact right angles*. Now drop a plumb-line from A to C, then do the same from B to D, at the other end; next stretch the line from C to D, saw cuts down to these two lines, every 6 inches or 9 inches apart;

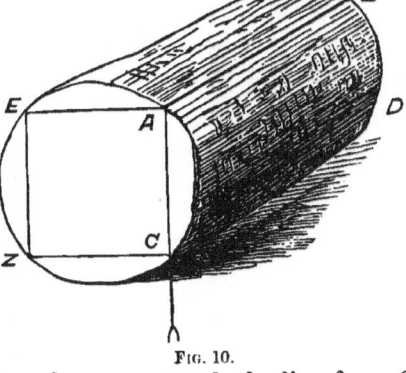

FIG. 10.

then take an axe and knock off the whole slice, finishing all smooth with the adze. You have now got one side squared, and that is sufficient for the ground-plates; but if you want a square post, then drop the plumb-line from A to E, do the same at the other end, stretch the chalk line and smooth off as before; then treat the sides, C to Z and Z to E, in the same way. Do the other ground plates the same way, and then mark a chalked line down the centre of this flattened side; this is for a guide for the mortise-holes that you will have to put in for the other posts. The top wall-plates will require squaring on two sides—that is, above and below; mark also the centre line for the mortise-holes in them as well. Now take the four large corner-

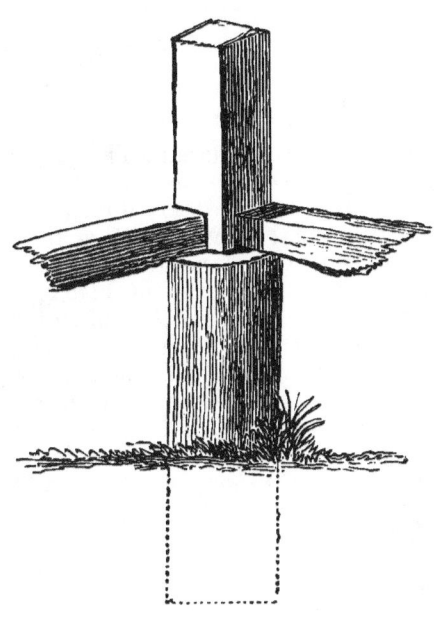

FIG. 12.

posts and square two sides of them for 9 feet of their length; but these two squared sides are not to be opposite ones like the wall-plates, but the *two adjoining* sides that are intended to face inwards (see fig. 12); the two main centre posts square on *three* inner sides; the fifteen smaller uprights square on the two *opposite* sides, and for their whole length. On the top and bottom of these latter posts cut a projecting tongue, 3 inches x 2 inches and 4 inches long; this is to fit into the corresponding mortise-hole in the ground and wall-plates; the distance these are to be apart is optional, according to the doors and windows you intend to have; but I have marked on the plan allowing for two

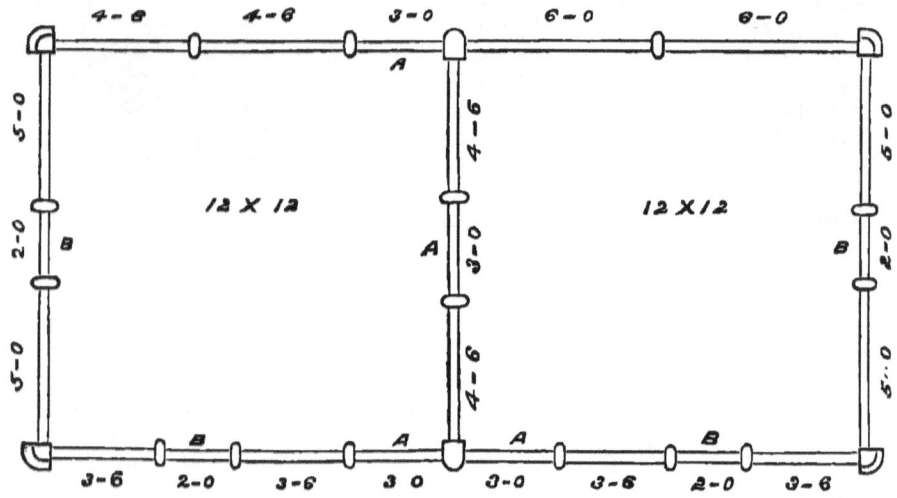

PLAN SHOWING POSITION OF POSTS FOR TWO-ROOMED HORIZONTAL SLAB-HUT.

doors and two windows to each room, for there is nothing like plenty of openings in our hot climate. The top of the four corner and two centre posts you must also tongue, but make it longer, say 6 inches.

Now erect the four corner and two centre posts, putting them 2 feet 6 inches in the ground; try them with the plumb-line that they are perfectly upright, also that they are perfectly level, by placing a straight-edged batten on the top of the posts, and a spirit-level on the top of it; then put on the wall-plates (having first mortised the holes for the tongues of the posts to go into), but do not nail them as yet, and ram the earth firmly around the posts. Next place a short stump (12 inches thick) between each of these upright posts, let it be 2 feet in the ground, and the top sawn off level with the squared shoulder of the main posts—that is, it will project 6 inches above ground; then fit the ground-plate so as to rest, at each of its ends, on the two shoulders, and supported in the middle by the stump. The under side of this plate being round, you will have to trim the ends so as to let it sit firm and level; then nail with stout nails or, better still, bore an inch auger hole through the plate and into the corner posts and stump, and plug with a hardwood treenail to fit; do the same with the other ground-plates; then mark off and mortise the holes for the smaller posts, place them in, lift up the wall-plate, and slip the tongues into the holes in it, and finally nail it down. Fix cross-pieces for the doors and windows, and also put two additional ground-plates in each room; these must have their upper side squared, and must rest on stumps put 2 feet in the ground.

Now start putting the flooring down—it will make the rest of the work easier to be got at; if you can 'ford it, get sawn boards for the floor; if not, you must use slabs adzed smooth; but they are nasty things for this work, and the women folk do not like them, for they are hard to scrub, and never look as if they had been washed; deal boards I do not recommend, for the white ants will eat them to pieces in a twelvemonth. You can now begin putting in the slabs. To do this, nail on the flat side of every upright, and extending from the ground-plate to the wall-plate, two battens 1 inch square, leaving a space of 1½ inches between them; thus making a groove of that width, into which the two ends of the slabs will slide; but, in order to get the slabs in, one of these battens must not come higher than about 1 foot from the wall-plate. Now take a slab, cut it to the exact width between the pair of uprights you are working at, lift it up over the shorter batten, and let it drop down the groove to the ground-plate; then drop another on the top of it, and so on till the panel is completed. An objection I have heard raised against horizontal slabs is that they let the wet drip through the joints, but if you take the trouble to bevel the edges as shown in fig. 13, they will be as water-tight as a weather-board house, for their own weight will keep them close, no matter how much they may shrink; but be sure you put the bevel the right way, or the water will run in instead of out. Never mind fitting the top slab close to the wall-plate, for there will soon be a space there, through the shrinkage going on, and you can fill it up at any after time by putting in a narrow slab. Finish all the other panels in the same way, and the hut will then be ready for the roof.

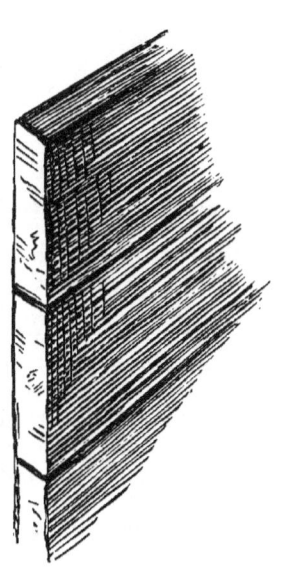

Fig. 13.

ROOFING THE HUT.—If you can afford to buy galvanised corrugated iron, I strongly advise you to roof with it and not with shingles, for these reasons: it never rots; it is fire-proof against the burning sparks of a bush fire; it lets in no rain, even after the longest drought; and the water caught from off it is the best you can possibly have for drinking and for all domestic purposes, including dairy work, and will keep sweet and clean in tanks under ground, whereas the water from a shingle roof is always more or less dirty, discoloured, and quite unfit for washing butter or for dairy purposes. Iron also requires a lighter roof, fewer rafters, and very few battens, and is more quickly and easily put on. Still, shingles have their advantages, and many people prefer them: first, you can get them on your own land, or on adjoining Crown lands, so that there is no money out of pocket to procure them—only labour expended; they are also cooler in summer and warmer in winter than sheet-iron; in addition to which they have this great advantage, they are *hail-proof*, for it has several times occurred in this colony that a heavy hailstorm has completely riddled an iron roof, so much so as to necessitate a new one. Another advantage: a strong gale of wind sometimes comes and whips off the whole of the iron roof at one blow, whereas shingles can only go one at a time; so I will give you a few "hints" as to how to put them on.

In the centre, and on the top side of each of the two ends, and of the middle wall-plates, mortise a hole for, and fix in, a "king-post" not less than 4 feet long by 4 inches square; cut slots in the top of these posts, 3 inches deep by 1 inch broad, so as to enable you to fix along them a 6-inch by 1-inch board, 24 feet long, as a ridge. The rafters will require to be 7 feet 6 inches long; do not use round saplings for these, but split them out of the butt of a tree, just as if you were splitting rails; have them not less than 2 inches thick by 4 inches deep, and the top edge must be adzed straight if it is not already so. Bevel the two ends so that they fit nicely to the ridge and to the wall-plate, to both of which they must be nailed; place them not more than 2 feet 6 inches apart, always having them in pairs—that is, opposite each other. On these nail sawn battens 3 inches by $1\frac{1}{2}$ inch; if the roof is for iron only four on each side will be wanted; but if for shingles, you will want three to every shingle's length—that is, fifteen or sixteen on each side. If you cannot get sawn battens you will have to adze down saplings or split as long lengths as you can out of some easy-splitting tree, but you must adze these smooth, for it is *essential* to a *shingle roof* that the battens be all level and smooth; also they *must* be put on *perfectly horizontal* and *equidistant*—then you will have no trouble with the shingles. As I suppose your shingles are 18 inches long, a batten must be put every 6 inches, leaving, if the batten is 3 inches wide, a space also of 3 inches between each one. As a new hand at bush work it may, perhaps, surprise you to be told that *one* nail is only required for each shingle—it is quite sufficient; if you put *two*, you will probably split the shingle, for they *will* curl up or contract with dry weather, and expand with wet, do what you will, and the one nail allows them to do this without cracking. Do not attempt to drive the nail without first boring a hole for it, and bore this hole $4\frac{1}{2}$ inches from the top end. You can do this with a gimlet and each shingle separately, but you will find it a most awful bother, and if the shingles are thick and at all seasoned (as they should be) your wrist will be pretty badly strained before you have done; so buy a brace and half-a-dozen bits (it is a tool you will always be wanting for all sorts of jobs), and fix a slab upright in the ground; on this, just about the height of your waist, fix a box or frame that will hold three or four shingles at once; bore a hole through this, exactly where you want the hole to be through the shingle; then slip in some shingles, and by using the brace and bit you will get through half-a-dozen in the time of doing one with a gimlet, and the hole will always be in the same and right place of each individual shingle.

To shingle a roof requires considerable skill and some practice before you can do it properly, but these "hints" may perhaps teach you sufficiently to enable you to experiment upon your own house if you like. So take as many shingles as will make one row the length of the hut, put them in bundles of three or four into your box or frame, bore a hole through them, take them out, turn them over, put them in again and bore another hole at the opposite end, then saw them into two, exactly across the middle; thus making two shingles 9 inches long out of each one, and with a hole bored exactly in the middle of them—these are for the first or bottom row, and also for the last or top row. Now take these halves and nail them on to the lowest batten (which must be at the very end of the rafters), putting them quite close together and letting them project exactly 3 inches. Do not put the whole row on at once, but work upwards in breadth just as wide as you can conveniently stretch over, commencing at the right-hand corner as you face the building. Now take a full-length shingle and place it over the joint between the two halves (so as to completely cover this joint), and nail it; the top of this will be just up to, but not on, batten No. 3 (see fig. 14), and the nail will be in the centre of batten No. 2. Then put on another full-length, the top of which comes up exactly to, but not on, batten No. 4; the top of the next batten will in the same way come up to batten No. 5, and so on up to the ridge, where the half-shingles will be again wanted to finish off with.

Fig. 14.

If the shingles are all one length (as you can easily make them) and the battens all exactly a true distance apart (as they ought to be), you will find no difficulty at all in the matter; the only care required will be, as the shingles are not all one width, to choose such ones as will properly protect the joint of the lower row by covering it with the upper one well on to each side. Notice that batten No. 2 is 6 inches from No. 1; all the others are just 3 inches apart. When you have both sides done, put on a ridging of galvanised iron if you can get it; if not, then one formed of two sawn hardwood boards, 6 inches by 1 inch, nailed saddle-ways together, and nailed also to the top battens. A roof covered with shingles is a great weight, and has a tendency to bulge out the walls; so nail a light batten inside from each rafter to its opposite, making a figure A of each pair; also put diagonal stays, as shown previously on bark huts. For the gable ends the best way is to nail up with sawn boards, but if you cannot obtain them, choose thin slabs and nail to the rafters and the king-posts, cutting the ends to the slope of the roof as required. If you cannot afford to buy windows, a shutter made out of old deal cases does very well, for in our fine climate windows nearly always are wanted open; as long as you have the power to close them at will when a storm comes, or on a cold night, that is all that is absolutely necessary. Doors also are best made of deal; when made out of slabs—as can easily be done—they are but clumsy things. The fireplace for a slab hut can be made exactly like the plan I gave for putting up bark chimneys, only substituting slabs for bark.

You have now a comfortable weatherproof house over you—one that is warm in winter and cool in summer—and, if well and carefully put up, by no means unsightly to look at. You can, at your leisure, add a verandah and other rooms, not forgetting a comfortable kitchen for your wife.

Fig. 15.

I have dwelt fully upon this slab hut because it is a type by which you can put up stables, barn, milking-house or woolshed—the only difference being in the size; the same method of plan and work applies to all.

DOORS AND WINDOWS FOR A HUT.—I purpose now giving you a few hints as to how you can, even at a very trifling expense, make your new home quite comfortable—that is, if you are at all a handy man with tools; and any man, no matter what his trade may have been in the old country, can easily acquire the little skill requisite for Australian bush carpentering, if he only tries to do so. I strongly urge you to acquire this skill, for you can then, in a thousand and one ways, make your house snug and pretty, your fences secure, the barn and stables weatherproof; in fact, your farm will be comfortable and complete; and what is success but comfort?

I have not much to say about doors and windows, but a hint or two may perhaps help you. In our fine climate windows can well be dispensed with until you have money to spare. A wooden shutter made out of old packing-case wood will be quite sufficient protection from the weather, for it will be seldom, even if you have a window, that it will not be left open, especially if your hut has a verandah round it. If you are close to town and can get glazed sashes cheap and without trouble, then do so by all means, but if your selection is far in the interior, and carriage expensive, then do without, using only a shutter.

Doors can be made of deal or other light wood. If you can get sawn timber they are easily made by nailing a board across the top, middle, and bottom of the requisite number of boards cut to the length of the doorway; hang it with stout T hinges, they are the best for all bush-house work. If you are located where you cannot get sawn boards, then you must split light thin slabs and use them instead; but a slab door is heavy, and apt to drop at the end, so nail a batten as a diagonal stay from the heel to the top corner, and hang it the same way as I shall by-and-by tell you to do when making a crane for the fire-place. Doors are frequently made out of a sheet of bark fastened on to a frame of saplings, but they are ugly-looking things and only fit for a bark hut.

In the far interior, where there is no timber to split or to get bark off, an old bag nailed on to a frame is what you may use, and it does very well for the primitive huts of our pioneer settlers; of course it is only a makeshift till better can be got, but the art of contriving "makeshifts" is one of the most useful of accomplishments that a new selector can possess.

HUT FURNITURE.—A capital stretcher for one person, when living in a tent or hut with earthen floor, can be made in a few minutes, if a couple of old flour bags are at hand, thus: Cut two light saplings 7 feet long and 2 inches thick, take off the bark, smooth down the knots, slit a hole in the two bottom corners of the bag, and run the sticks through the mouth of it and through the corner slits; thread the other bag on in the same way; now cut two logs, about 1 foot thick and 1 foot wider than the width of the bag, place these logs one for the head and one for the foot of the stretcher, lay the projecting ends of the saplings on them, bore a 1-inch hole in the logs just inside of each spar, and put a peg in; this keeps them from coming together when your weight is on the bag. By this simple plan you can keep yourself off the frequently damp, if not wet, floor of a tent, and so save yourself from future years of rheumatic pains, fever, piles, etc. Although the Australian climate is mild, and exposure does not tell so soon on the constitution as in Europe, yet it does eventually tell; and my advice to you is—although you may be young and strong now, yet never neglect taking precautions against ill-health if you are able to do so; do not, except when travelling, sleep on the ground just because you are too lazy to make a stretcher.

FIG. 16.

Instead of resting the stretcher on logs, you can put stout forked saplings in the ground, well ram the earth around them, and put the ends of the stretcher spars in these forks (see fig. 17), then nail on a head-board.

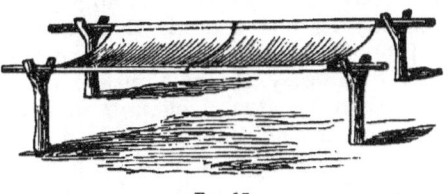

FIG. 17.

All through these pages I have presumed that you did not select your land till you were married, for the woman's skill is necessary to the successful working of your farm; not that I advocate her working in the fields—that is man's work—but in the dairy, the

poultry-yard, the garden, and in cooking you a good meal, she is
required before you can call
yourself successful (of course
I am now only speaking in a
practical sense); so devote a
few days to making her the
various household things I am
now going to tell you about.

First make a CRANE to the
fireplace. For the want of
this many a woman gets her
foot scalded, or her clothes
catch fire, or she gets a nasty
sprain, besides being annoyed
all day long just for the want
of this simple contrivance.
The heavy pot in which the
meat is boiled, the large boiler
full of clothes, etc., are no
joke for the wife to lift on
and off, so make her a crane;
it is a well-known old English
kitchen convenience, but in
Australia it is seldom seen;
yet in a bush hut, with its large
fireplace, it is absolutely necessary. Fig. 18 shows how it
is made and fitted to the fireplace. Get two pieces of hardwood about 5 feet long, mortise the end of one into the

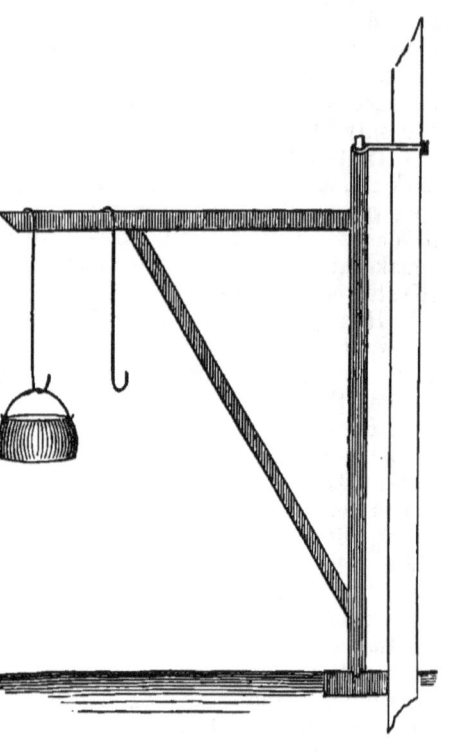

FIG. 18.

face of the other and put a diagonal stay, as in the sketch; make a
round tenon at the bottom of the heel-post, and bore a hole in a
block of wood which will just fit this tenon; sink this block level with
the stones of the fireplace floor, and close to the right-hand edge of
the fireplace; on it the crane will work. The top of the heel-post
must also be rounded off, and a ½-inch iron bolt must be got from the
blacksmith, one end of which must have a *round* eye, into which the
top tenon is put. A hole is then bored quite through the corner-post
of the chimney, the bolt pushed through, and the nut screwed on; it
will then be strong enough to stand the weight of all the pots that
can possibly be hung on it, and all the wife has to do to get them on
or off is to swing the crane to her. They can then be easily got at,
as she is away from the fire. A strip of zinc tacked on to the underneath side will hinder the wood charring, no matter how big the fire.

TABLES, CHAIRS, AND BEDSTEADS you can easily and cheaply
make out of old deal packing cases. In the old country it is very
likely deal boxes were valuable and but seldom seen by you, but out
here they are everywhere knocking about, and you can buy them at a

very low price from any country store or town shop. Cases that originally contained jam tins, fruit bottles, brandy and other spirits, are the handiest sizes, but the larger cases that once contained drapery are useful for breaking up, and for wardrobes, shelves, &c. It is astonishing what a variety of makeshifts can be constructed, by exercising a little ingenuity, out of the rigid form of a rectangular box. A handy small SIDE TABLE can be made in a few minutes, thus: Take a brandy case and at each corner *inside* nail four legs of ½-inch board, as long as you want the table to be high (see fig. 19):

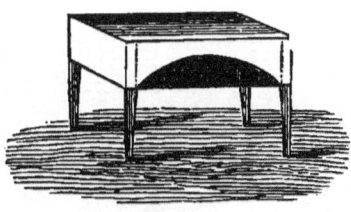

FIG. 19.

by making the legs shorter you have a nice light stool for the children to sit on; by using a gin case and nailing on the top again after you have fitted the legs, and cutting out one side into a half circle (see fig. 19), you will have a strong and light stool, upon which the wife can put her tubs when washing, and inside of which she can stow away scrubbing or blacking brushes, floorcloths, or any other untidy-looking things. If you want a *bigger table* still, then break up a drapery case and nail some of the smoothest boards on to the top, letting the ends and sides project some distance from the top.

A LARGE KITCHEN TABLE can be made by taking *two* cases, a little longer than before, nailing legs of inch wood at the inside corners, as in the previous table; place them 5 feet apart—outside measurement—and nail smooth boards, 6 feet long, from one to the other. The width of the top should not be more than 3 feet, and as the sides should project 4 inches, the boxes will

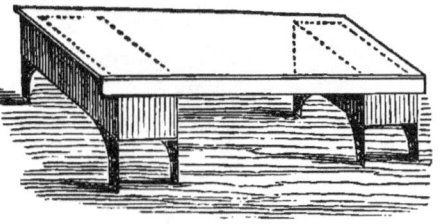

FIG. 20.

only want to be about 2 feet 4 inches long, by any depth and width. The ends of the boards should project 6 inches, and a side board should be nailed from box to box, as shown in fig. 20. By nailing on the tops of the boxes again after fixing the legs, and cutting out the semi-circle in one side, as you did in the washing-stool, a capital shelf or cupboard is made of each box, in one of which the wife can keep her tablecloth, etc., and the other will hold your farm books, accounts, and papers, and be always handy.

A CAPITAL SOFA can be made in exactly the same way as the table, except that one box must come flush with the ends of the top boards, and a head-board, 9 inches broad, must be nailed so as to keep the pillow or cushions on; the wife can cover the whole with chintz, and it will really look, and be, a nice piece of furniture.

Even a GOOD BEDSTEAD can be also made in this double-box manner, and inch battens nailed on the outside of each corner, carried up as high as is necessary, cross ones nailed to them, and so a mosquito net can be hung all round (fig. 21). It is better in the case of the sofa and bedstead to nail the side-board lower down than you did when making the table.

The old boxes out of which I showed you how to make sofa, bedstead, tables, and stools, can be turned into an EASY CHAIR in a very few minutes and with very little trouble, thus: Take an old gin case and nail on to the two ends the battens as shown in the sketch (fig. 22), nail cross pieces from one to the other at the top, and then nail the two short battens that project out behind; these hinder the chair tipping backwards when you are lounging in it. Fill a flour bag with dry grass, tack it all round the top of the box and extending up the side battens to the crosspiece and tack it firmly there. Your part of the work is now done; but get the wife to make a cover of chintz or holland that will go over the whole, but which must not be fastened permanently, or it cannot be got off to be washed. It will not be long before your wife makes this her favourite seat, for a more comfortable one for sewing or reading in could not be bought out of a shop. I have known these chairs to be retained in the drawing-room even after the owner had become a rich man, the mayor of the town, and member of our Legislative Assembly.

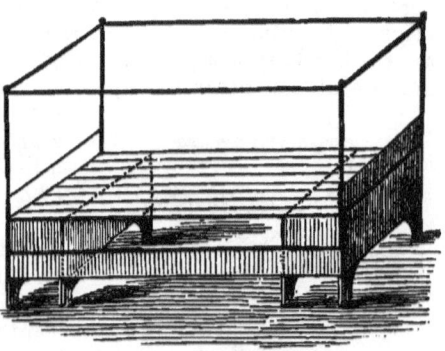

FIG. 21.

FIG. 22.

FIG. 23.

Another easily constructed chair I take a sketch of from the *American Agriculturist;* the drawing (fig. 23) explains itself.

SQUATTER'S OR VERANDAH CHAIR.—Then there is the squatter's or verandah chair, which is so very comfortable to rest and smoke in, but which takes up too much room to be used indoors. It is made thus: Take two pieces of wood about 4 feet 6 inches long, and 2 inches by 2 inches or thereabouts in thickness, mortise cross-pieces at the top, and about 6 inches from the bottom, thus making a frame (see fig. 24); then make a similar but a smaller frame for the back legs—this must be just wide enough to slip inside the larger frame; now put a half-inch bolt through the two where they touch or cross each other; then fasten a piece of rope on each side as shown; this takes the whole strain and allows the chair to be folded up when required. The seat is made by tacking canvas or bagging from the top cross-piece to the cross-piece of the shorter frame, letting it hang slack, or "belly down" as much as is thought most comfortable; do not tack the edges of the canvas to the side pieces.

Fig. 24.

A simpler form of this chair is constructed thus:—Make the larger of the two frames, as above, but let the lower cross-piece be 1 foot from the ends; then nail with strong tacks canvas, as before, from top to bottom, again letting it hang down loose in the middle; the chair is then made. By resting the top against the side of the house, any inclination can be given to it, and in it, under your own verandah, covered with vines and passion-fruit, can be spent your well-earned Sunday afternoon's rest (see fig 25).

You can make forms and stools by the dozen, and in a very short time, if you are splitting slabs, by choosing a stout sound one, cutting it to the length you want, smoothing the top face, boring four holes, one near each corner, and driving in light round saplings for the legs, giving them an incline outwards; cut a nick in the end that goes into the hole and drive in a wedge, so as to keep these legs from falling out when they get dry and shrink.

Fig. 25.

MEAT SAFES.—One of the most necessary pieces of furniture required by the settler in any of the Australian colonies is a meat safe. In the summer time both the small house-flies and the larger flesh or blow-flies are in myriads; the latter deposit living maggots, so that meat left uncovered is unfit for eating in an hour's time; ants, too,

G

in some districts are always on the forage for something good, and if only one finds out your eatables he tells the others, and when your next meal-time comes round you find everything smothered with these disgusting little insects; so a meat safe is necessary, even although you may be but living in a tent; I will therefore describe and sketch two or three sorts.

The simplest and easiest made is this: Take a clean flour bag with no holes in it, and hang it up to the ridge pole of your tent by a string fastened to one of the bottom corners, and by another string placed on the same side seam but about 6 inches from the mouth of the bag; then put in a board some 7 inches wide, 6 inches less in length than the bag; this flattens out the bottom, making a sort of shelf; put in your meat dish and anything else requiring protection, tie up the mouth of the bag closely, and this safe is both fly and ant proof. It can with advantage be hung from the branches of a low tree, it will then get more air than in the tent, for its fault is that it is too close (see fig. 26).

FIG. 26.

For indoors, a better form of the foregoing is one that I have myself used for years; it is simply made thus:—Take a board 12 inches wide and, say, 2 feet long, bore a gimlet-hole close to each corner; get two pieces of common fencing wire 4 feet long, also a light batten 1 inch × ¾ inch the same length as the board; bore a hole close to each end, thread the two wires each through one of these holes, slip them along till the centre of the wire is reached—that is, 2 feet; bend down the ends, insert them through the holes in the plank, and clench. Now tack mosquito-netting over the whole, leaving enough slack at one end to tie it, the same as you did the bag safe. It can either be hung up or not as desired, and it makes a nice airy perfectly fly-proof safe; it is proof also against the larger sort of ants, but not against the disgusting little black ones.

But neither of these are safe against rats or mice; so get a sound strong, but not too big, zinc-lined drapery case from the nearest store, take out the zinc lining, and cut out a large piece from the centre of the two ends and the back; if you have not got a small saw you can do this by boring auger holes all round the piece; it will then easily knock out, and you can smooth off with a rasp or chisel. Now cut the zinc into sheets, and puncture very small holes in it with a sharp nail, till each sheet is perfectly riddled, then tack them on to the outside of the wooden box, so covering the large holes cut in it. A door can be made out of the spare top of the case, but cut it smaller, so that it will fit easily inside; hang it with a pair of butt hinges, and tack all round the edges some calico, flannel, or a strip of leather, so as to make a perfectly tight fit when the door is closed. Now nail four legs to the case of 1 inch × 2 inch board, and place these legs each in an old jam or salmon tin, which you must keep full of water; see that everything is clear of the wall, and you will have a rough but serviceable safe that neither rats, mice, ants, nor flies can get into.

Of course if you are near town you can buy a good safe cheap enough, or you can buy the perforated zinc and make a frame one according to your skill; my directions are only for anyone who may be located far in the interior.

A capital form of *safe for hanging meat*, such as a whole sheep just slaughtered, or the parts of a bullock you do not intend to salt down, is made thus: Get a piece of round board, or rather nail boards together till you can cut out a circle 2 feet or even 3 feet in diameter, according to the quantity of meat you are likely to have at once; hang this circle—the top of a cask will do—by a strong hook or piece of twisted fencing wire placed in the centre; then screw in hooks—wire will do—from the *under side*, and tack all around the edge of the circular top a clean flour bag with the bottom cut out, but if you can get osnaburg or cheese-cloth use it instead of the bag, for it is more porous to the air, and you can make it to hang down low enough to cover a whole sheep. The meat is hung to the hooks and the bag tied closely below it (see fig. 27).

FIG. 27.

Having pointed out to you, the new comer, the necessity for your learning Australian occupations before selecting land; having shown you how to fall trees, to split slabs, rails, posts, and shingles; to strip bark; to put up tents, bark or slab huts; how to go about selecting land; the best situation for the house, and how to cheaply but comfortably furnish it, I conclude.

USEFUL GARDENING OPERATIONS.

PLANT PROPAGATION.

ALL who take an interest in gardening are anxious to succeed, to some extent at least, in the propagation of favourite and valuable plants. The art of propagation is in itself exceedingly interesting, and in the attention it demands to its many details calls for the exercise of watchfulness, patience, and skill to achieve success; and even if the propagator aims at nothing more than keeping his own borders properly supplied and furnishing an occasional plant of something choice to a friend, the amount of gratification thereby realised is very satisfying. To propagate successfully, the laws of nature operative in connection with plant growth must be understood and obeyed. Nature does the work when we supply the circumstances and materials for her to operate upon. The necessity of being able to strike cuttings, put down layers, insert a few buds, or do a little grafting occasionally is obvious even on the ground of economy; for there are few amateurs, especially in these colonies, whose circumstances warrant them in running to a nurseryman or florist for every little thing they require; and the fact of acquiring the knowledge needful in this way will make them all the more enthusiastic in horticultural pursuits. With the intention of enabling the reader to do this, the following directions and necessary illustrations are furnished, which should make the work comparatively easy to all.

STRIKING CUTTINGS.

Under favourable circumstances most plants may be readily propagated from cuttings. A cutting is a portion of a plant capable of emitting roots, and of becoming an individual plant similar to its parent. The circumstances necessary to effect this are first a proper preparation of the cuttings; and in addition to this the preparation of a suitable compost to strike them in, a proper temperature, and a certain and regular supply of moisture. The rooted cutting is simply an extension of the parent, having precisely the same habits, and requiring the same treatment in every particular. The operator needs to bear in mind that until roots are formed no healthy growth of foliage can take place; and consequently the object should be to promote the speedy formation of roots before there is any foliage to make demands upon them. Unless artificial means—such as propagating houses or hot beds—are employed for striking cuttings, early autumn is the best season for putting them in; because then the soil is usually warmer than the atmosphere, which encourages the formation of roots rather than foliage. In this hot and frequently dry climate it is of the first importance when striking cuttings in the open air that they be inserted the greater part of their entire length in the ground. Fig. 1 represents a cutting of a vine, and the dotted line shows the surface of the soil in which it is planted.

If anything let the cutting be deeper than this rather than shallower, always supposing the soil in which they are required to grow is broken up to a sufficient depth below the bottom of the cutting to give it a chance. In speaking of vine propagation, it may be as well to state here that vine cuttings are best planted out where they are to remain. The vine plant sends out long roots right away from the stem : and all the care imaginable in removing them afterwards cannot be successful in lifting even a tithe of the roots. As a rule a rooted vine, planted at the same time and in the same soil as the cutting, will not be any further forward at the end of the first year than the cutting, and frequently does not recover the vigour lost at the time of transplanting, but is left behind by the cutting. The illustration given here will also convey an accurate idea of how a vine cutting should be prepared. The principle of making

Fig 1. a clean cut immediately below a bud is helpful in encouraging the formation of roots, and should be followed in preparing cuttings of every description for the same reason. Fig. 2 shows a rose cutting prepared and planted; the dotted lines showing the depth it should be inserted in the soil. Particular attention should be paid to the depth at which rose, and, in fact, any cutting should be planted. It would be better to err in having the cuttings too much in the ground rather than too much above it.

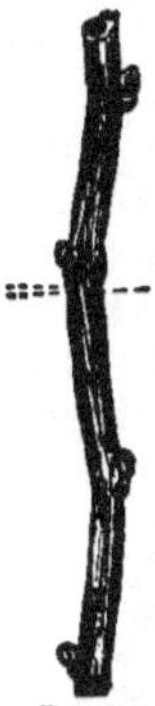

The cuttings should be made of young but ripe wood, not more than 8 inches long; and as they are prepared they should be planted, opening out trenches the length of the bed to the required depth as nearly as possible, and inserting the cuttings. Then fill in a little soil and firm it well with the foot; and if the weather be dry give a good watering and fill in the remainder of the soil leaving a level surface. Be sure Fig. 2.
and firm the soil before wetting it, or if the soil be at all heavy it will cake and that will hinder the formation of roots.

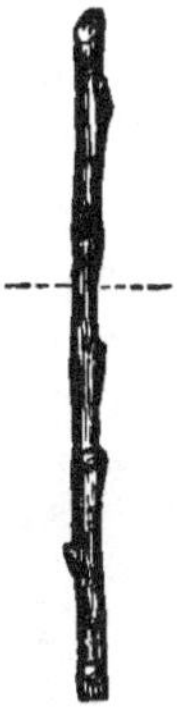

For the first few days after planting it is necessary, in hot weather, to provide a temporary shading, such as some light brushwood or boughs. These can be occasionally removed to admit light and air. Fig. 3 shows how mulberry and fig cuttings are prepared and planted.

Where cuttings of any plant or plants prove to be shy in emitting roots, it is now becoming a practice to neatly fit a small piece of a fibrous root into the lower end of the cutting before planting and secure it with a bit of matting. In doing so the root should in the first place be of the same nature as

Fig. 3.   the cutting—the apple root for an apple cutting—and it should also be fitted together, bark to bark, so that a union as in grafting may be effected and a flow of sap thereby made possible.

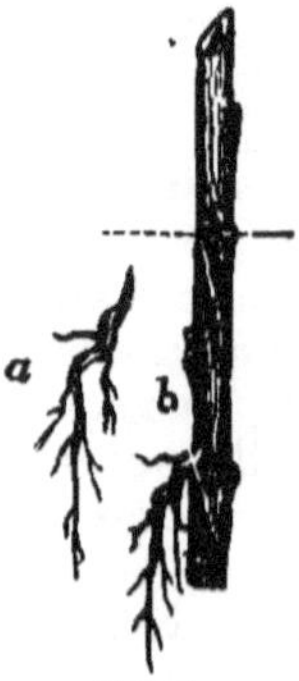

Fig. 4 represents a cutting of an apple tree with a small bit of fibrous root neatly inserted.

That portion of the woodcut marked *a* represents the root prepared for insertion; and *b* gives a clear idea of the root secured in place and the cutting planted. This method of propagating blight-proof apples is very commonly in use amongst nurserymen, and is found to be very effective while it is also simple. The principle being a good one will bear almost indefinite extension, and when our horticultural friends meet with plants which are too slow in forming roots for themselves, let them make an application of the principle and learn for themselves the extent or limit of its usefulness. In all cases, however, the root must be freshly taken from a plant of the same species, and the inner bark of root and cutting must be fitted neatly together as in grafting to enable a union between the two to be effected. Fig. 5 represents a cutting of cypress prepared for striking, and inserted in the soil.

FIG. 4.

It will be seen that the cutting is taken from the extreme point of a branch, and that two or three leaflets are cut cleanly off from the base to allow its insertion in the soil to the required depth. It is usual to prick these cuttings thickly into flower-pots containing an admixture of loam sand and peat well mixed and broken up, and to stand the pots in a close frame, or better still, where they can feel the influence of a little bottom heat. Only in very favourable and exceptional circumstances can cuttings of the cypress family be expected to grow in the open border. Then again we have another class of cuttings, such as the pink, carnation, and picotee, which require special treatment; and the following illustration, Fig. 6, will give a pretty correct idea of how it should be done.

FIG. 5.

Pipings which have never thrown up a flower stem are the portions to select, and a few leaves from the base should be cut clean away leaving a portion of the stem bare, sufficient, at any rate, to allow of its insertion in the soil to a sufficient depth to escape the possibility of being readily dried. Cuttings like this, however, require more care and attention than can be bestowed upon them in the open borders; and may therefore be either inserted moderately thick in pots and stood in a close and shaded frame, or they may be struck in proper soil in the open ground with the protection of a shaded hand-light over them. Many soft-wooded plants, such as antirrhinums, carnations, chrysanthemums, coleus, dianthus, gaillardias, lobelias, fuchsias, pelargoniums, petunias, penstemons, Indian pinks, salvias, and verbenas can be struck in this climate, during the autumn season of the year, by adopting the following methods: Make a bed the size required somewhere in the open border, that is as far

FIG. 6.

removed as possible from the influence of growing trees or shrubs of any kind; a bed 4 feet wide by 10 feet long will suffice for nearly a couple of hundred cuttings. Make the surface soil rich, light, and porous, by a free admixture of sand and wood rubbish—old sawdust is as good as anything that can be had. Prepare an artificial shading of boughs to exclude the sun's rays, and to shelter from the drying westerly winds. Having done this, proceed at once as follows:—Open a trench at one end of the bed deep enough to insert your cuttings; lay them a few inches apart in the trench, and put back part of the soil against them, firming it with your foot; then saturate the soil with water, and fill up the trench smooth and level, leaving no more than a couple of inches of the cuttings above the surface. The cuttings themselves should be no more than 6 or 7 inches long and should be clean cut through at a joint at the base, and all the leaves cut smoothly from the stem below ground. The whole of the bed may be proceeded with similarly. Watch the bed for signs of failing moisture, and water only when needed, which, with proper shading, should not be oftener than once a week. For all the plants mentioned above, cuttings are best taken from the growing tops of the plants, when not too soft, but more or less matured. Fuchsias and some of the more tender plants might be treated thus:—Put plenty of good draining material, such as charcoal, for a few inches in the bottom of a large-sized flower-pot; then fill to within 3 inches of the surface with good sandy light compost; prick in your cuttings thickly and carefully, plunge the pot to the rim in the cutting bed, and cover the pot with glass, either in strips or in one piece, as most convenient. Keep moist, but avoid over watering, and when moisture collects on the glass wipe it off. Small healthy cuttings of many things are easily struck in this way, without bottom heat, and the best time to set about it is before the soil heat is gone at the end of summer or the beginning of the autumn months. Closely related to the above methods of striking cuttings is the practice, very common among nurserymen, of raising plants of any choice vine by simply inserting single eyes prepared as below, and placing them in a flower-pot or shallow earthen pan of clean, sharp, fine sand.

To enable a prompt start being made the buds should be pressed firmly to the depth of half an inch in the sand, which must be kept just firm with moisture and then the pot or pan must be closed in with a bell-glass, or a sheet of window glass large enough to cover the top of the pan, until the buds burst. If properly managed they soon start to grow; and when they are sufficiently rooted, the young plants will require to be potted off singly into a good fibrous loam, and encouraged to grow until strong enough to plant out permanently. They must not be allowed to suffer from lack of moisture, or being so small the little life sap they contain will disappear and the buds become useless. A 6-inch pot will afford ample space for the insertion of six or eight buds. The advantage of this method consists in enabling the propagator to raise a plant from every bud of any choice or rare vine; and with the convenience of a close frame or a hot-bed, the plan is a very reliable one. The buds should be taken from shoots of the previous year's growth.

BUDDING.

This is a very useful and interesting method of propagation, easily applied to desirable varieties of fruit trees and many flowering plants. It is but seldom that any other process is used with the rose, except cuttings: and as the art of budding is the same in all cases, the rose will serve to explain and illustrate the work. In contradistinction to grafting, which is done in the spring, budding is attended to while the plant is in full growth and the bark parts cleanly from the wood. So far as the rose is concerned the work may be done at any time through the summer when the bark runs well; but with other trees it is customary to do it about, or a little after, midsummer. In addition to the bark separating freely from the wood, the buds for insertion must be obtained from ripened shoots of the season's growth, showing full and plump but dormant buds. Using the rose as an illustration, procure a cutting of ripened wood with plump and full

Fig. 5.

buds at the footstalk of every leaf, but not started. Fig. 5 will convey the best idea of how it should be prepared.

Then with a sharp budding knife cut out one of the buds with bark and wood attached in the form of a shield as in Fig. 6. Next cut the top of the bark square, and with the thin bone handle of the knife remove the inner slip of wood without injuring the germ of the bud. If the bud is fit to insert there will be no depression opposite the bud on the inner side, but the inner bark surface will be smooth or a trifle full where the eye of the bud is; if there is deep depression waste no time with it, but throw it away and proceed to prepare another. If the shield is ready it will appear like Fig. 7.

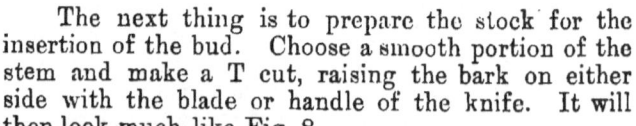

Fig. 7.   Fig. 6.

Fig. 9.   Fig. 8.

The next thing is to prepare the stock for the insertion of the bud. Choose a smooth portion of the stem and make a T cut, raising the bark on either side with the blade or handle of the knife. It will then look much like Fig. 8.

The shield of bark containing the bud is then slipped into position in the T cut, as shown in Fig. 8. Some soft tying material, such as strips of old calico, tape, or bass matting, are then used to tie in the bud, tying all in smoothly and evenly while missing the bud as in Fig. 9. In a few weeks union will be sufficiently effected for loosening the tie, and in the case of the rose, the stock must be shortened to within a little of the bud at the same time. With fruit trees and other shrubs the shortening should be done in winter, cutting in as closely as possible to the bud. Fig. 10 shows the young shoot starting from the bud and held in position by a tie; but the better plan is to secure a light stick to the stock and tie the growing bud to it; for unless something of the kind is done the wind is very apt to blow out the bud before a strong union is effected.

Another method of budding consists in taking a ring of bark from the stock, and preparing a ring of bark from the scion containing a bud to put into its place. Oranges and the citrus family generally may be budded in this way; and when neatly fitted and secured with a tie as in other cases with the eye of the bud uncovered, this method is very effective. As a rule, this way is followed with subjects the bark of which are brittle and stiff.

FIG. 10.

LAYERING.

This is another very effective method of propagating, and it is adapted to a very great variety of plants. Sometimes a vine cutting misses in a row in a vineyard, and by layering from the nearest vine in the spot where the plant is needed, the loss of time occasioned by transplanting is avoided. Valuable shrubs and ornamental trees, and many softwooded and herbaceous plants, such as pinks, carnations, and (in this climate) double petunias may be increased in this way. The process is simple enough; in some cases, all that is necessary being to peg down the shoot firmly into freshly dug soil, and draw an inch or two of earth over the portion pegged down, leaving only the point of the shoot above ground. In most cases, however, a twist is given to the branch to be layered, or a wound made in some way at the spot where the peg is fixed, which by causing sap to exude, hastens the period of rooting. Afterwards it is necessary to keep the ground moist, and to mulch the surface, and then the layer will take root. Rooting takes longer with hard-wooded plants than soft ones; and the less they are disturbed until they have taken root the better. Roses, camellias, azaleas, franciscas, magnolias, in fact any choice shrub and many fruit trees, may be propagated in this way. Mangoes have in numerous instances, been successfully multiplied by layering in Queensland. As a rule the best season of the year to do this work in is just as the growing season commences, and that is as the wet season sets in.

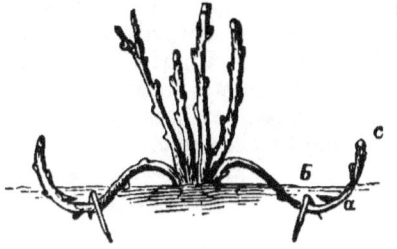

A good idea of the process will be formed by looking at the illustration given here. The best portions of any plant to layer are those which trail along the ground, as they more readily make roots than the upright shoots.

GRAFTING.

In nearly every branch of horticulture the great secret of success lies in doing seasonable work. There is in orchard operations a time to plant and a time to prune, a time to bud and a time to graft; and when these several necessary matters are attended to with a fair amount of skill and patience they are pretty sure to succeed. The time for grafting is early spring, about August and September, and to the new colonist, or the amateur who may be groping his way into the details of orchard work, a few practical hints will be useful.

It may be well to remark at the outset that experienced men in orchard work do not agree perfectly on all points. Every man who has an experience naturally relies more on it than on the experience of another who differs from him. And yet both may be equally correct while diverse, simply because their experiences have been acquired under different circumstances. Gardeners differ as to the best stock to work the pear upon, one preferring the quince to the pear, and another the reverse. Possibly both are right, the difference, may be, lying in the varying character of the soils and situations. Many a controversy rages through simply overlooking the important change of circumstances and surroundings between the two combatants. These remarks serve an important purpose at the present time, by fixing attention upon the widely different circumstances between horticultural work in the old country and the same in Queensland. A Queensland experience in these matters is what the individual cultivator, either in field or garden, must acquire to be a master of his art, and thereby command success. No European cultivator, however skilful, who has not sufficiently mastered the great underlying principles of his industry so as to apply them under widely different circumstances, can expect at the start in this colony to achieve success. These remarks apply to grafting as well as to all other operations in horticulture, and should be borne in mind by the new arrival.

Colonial experience has proved it necessary to depart in many particulars from old-country practices, and in nothing more than in the choice of stocks whereon to work trees for fruit-producing. The quince and hawthorn stocks for working pears upon have been tried, and proved failures; only pear stocks are worth planting under the climatic peculiarities of this colony. Oranges—which in some localities are thrifty and fruitful enough upon the lemon stock—are only worth cultivation here when worked on the orange. Grafting, which in the old country is almost invariably done at some distance above the ground, is found by colonial experience to be unsafe, and is condemned. These are a few of the leading particulars in which a deviation from old country practices has been found compulsory, owing to climatic and other differences between the two countries. Apprehension of these important truths at the outset of a new arrival's career will save much loss of time and money, and thus be exceedingly advantageous.

With reference to grafting, the first essential is to work scions only on stocks belonging to the same botanical order. Thus: the hawthorn, the pear, the apple, and the quince all belong to the same botanical order, and may be grafted upon each other with greater or less success; but neither of them could be grafted upon a cherry, plum, or peach. The peach, almond, and apricot can be grafted upon each other with great benefit under certain circumstances, but it would not be possible to graft any one of the foregoing fruits upon one of the citrus tribe, though any one of that order can be grafted upon stocks of its own family. There are several of our fruits known as plums that cannot be grafted upon the common English prune, and it is only waste of time and material to attempt it. There is one great principle in grafting that must be attended to. It lies in the fact that all growth in the exogenous trees—that is, such as grow on the outside every season—is in the "sapwood," or the liber. The object to be sought in grafting is to bring the edges of the liber, or inner bark, of both graft and stock into close contact with each other, so that the sap from the stock may be conducted fairly into the cells and channels of the graft, and thus a union effected and growth promoted. Another object sought by the skilful operator is to have the stock in a rather more forward state than the scion, so that when the work is done the scion may at once be urged into vitality by the ascending juices sent up by the stock. To secure this end the scions are generally taken off a month before they are wanted and put away in a shady place, partly burying them in cool and rather moist soil. In this hot climate branch grafting is not very successful, but when done close down to the ground, or beneath it, and then mulched over, it is as successful as anywhere else.

The colonial practice in raising young fruit trees is to obtain a supply of healthy and vigorous one or two year old seedling stocks, and in the position they have grown to head them down close to the ground, as at *a* Fig. 1; then a slice is cut smoothly off with a sharp knife, as at *b*, and a notch is cut in the surface of this, as at *c*.

FIG. 1.

The stock is then ready to receive the scion, which should have been previously taken from the young growth of the tree desired. The scion is then neatly cut to fit the stock, and one of the edges or bark of the scion must be brought exactly in contact with the edge or bark of the stock. When neatly fitted together thus they are secured in position by some soft tie, such as strips of calico, tape, or bass matting, and the whole is covered with prepared clay to exclude the air. The following illustrations will furnish ideas how the work is to be done.

Fig. 1, as said before, is the stock, headed down and prepared to receive the scion; Fig. 2 is the scion, prepared to fit into the stock; Fig. 3 shows the scion in position; Fig. 4 shows how the tie is to be put on; and Fig. 5 shows the work completed, and covered with clay.

The wedge or cleft system of grafting is the best and strongest; but some practitioners, instead of splitting down the stock with a chisel and fixing in the wedge-ended scion, make a double cut like a letter V with a fine-toothed saw, then trim off the roughness on the

FIG. 2.   FIG. 3.   FIG. 4.   FIG. 5.

liber with a very sharp knife, and insert the scion in the usual way. This prevents gumming in the stock lower down, which sometimes happens when it is split down; and the wound is more easily healed. The scion should be neatly cut wedge-shaped so as to fit the cleft all the way down; and, when fitted, the cleft and scion should be bandaged around with either a waxed cloth or with tempered clay or grafting wax.

Fig. 6 shows how this method is done: *a* being the wedge-shaped scion, and *b* the stock made ready and fitted with the scion or scions.

When the stocks are large, it is customary to insert two scions as shown in the engraving, and to cut one of them clean out again if both start to grow. This method is in general use to supersede old and worthless varieties; and where the stocks to be operated upon are large.

FIG. 6.

When the stock and scion are so nearly as possible of one size, a very perfect junction may be effected as shown by Fig. 7.

As in all other cases, when the stock and scion are neatly fitted together they are bound with a tie and clayed. Sometimes stocks are scarce to operate upon and then recourse may be had to slips of roots from a growing tree; always observing the rule given at the outset of this article, and providing the root from some tree of the same order. Fig. 8 shows how this may be done, and in general practice it is found to answer every purpose; giving good robust young trees in much the same time as is required when grafting in the ordinary way. Then there is the process of inarching, called also grafting by approach. This method is proved to be the only safe one for the mango, and, therefore, cannot well be

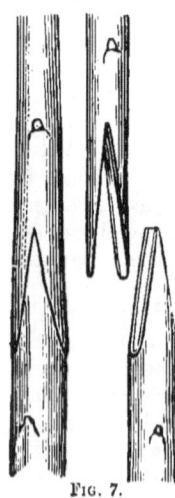

FIG. 7.

FIG. 8.

omitted here. The two growing plants, usually in pots, are brought together and an excision made in each, so as to leave an interlocking tongue, as at Fig. 9. As in other methods, the two are secured by some soft tie, and clayed over, and when union is effected, the head is cut away of the one not required, and the other left to fill its place. The stem of the desired variety is then severed below the junction, and in a short time the place of junction is concealed by new growth, and the desired end attained. Camellias and other plants difficult to treat by other methods are dealt with thus. Too much stress cannot be laid on the necessity of the barks of the scion and stock coming exactly together; for the success of the operation is entirely dependent upon this, and almost all failures, with the exception of such as are done unseasonably, may be attributed to carelessness in this particular. When the work is properly done the wound ought to be so well protected that no earth and very little, if any, air can gain access; and when this object has been secured the graft and stock should be covered up with a mound of earth or mulch. The old plan was to use clay finely worked and tempered with an equal part of horse or cow dung for covering over the bandages on grafts; but this occupies too much valuable time with the modern gardener, who secures a better medium in grafting wax, which is made of various substances. The most common and effective grafting wax is made of equal parts of resin, beeswax, and mutton fat, which is subjected to gentle heat, and then used for saturating long strips of old calico, which are rolled up on a stick, where they are kept until wanted for use. Another receipt for grafting wax will be found at the close of the next chapter on "Pruning."

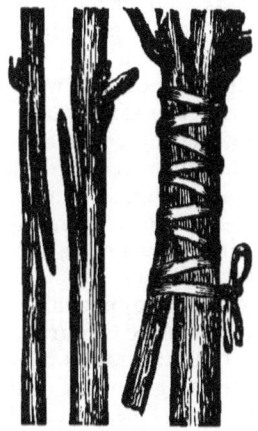

Fig 9.

PRUNING.

This is a matter about which much has already been written, and, considering the small amount of knowledge abroad upon the subject, much still requires to be written. As an art it is not done in imitation of nature, and yet, when properly executed it is not unnatural. There has been much controversy upon the subject amongst practical men, some of whom are altogether opposed to pruning; so that there are differences of opinion at the very outset even with reference to its advisability, besides the diverse opinions as to the manner in which the operation should be performed. A clear knowledge of the peculiarities of the tree or plant to be operated on is of primary importance. Pruning is not an art that can be taught like carpentry or masonry; every subject requiring to be operated on needs to have its individual peculiarities recognised, and the work done accordingly. For instance, there are roses and roses, each class of which requires a method of pruning adapted to its particular nature and habit. There are hybrid perpetual roses, Bourbons and hybrid Bourbons, tea-scented roses and noisettes, &c. All have different habits of growth and flowering, and require appropriate pruning. The Bourbons and teas are free bloomers, and make flowers as surely as they make wood ; but hybrid perpetuals, pillar or climbing roses, and noisettes, if cut severely, run into wood without blooming. Then there are distinct peculiarities of soil which make a difference of treatment necessary even with the same variety of rose or any other plant. Strong common sense, therefore, together with the knowledge of these differences and their cause, are the best aids to correct and useful pruning. There are, unfortunately, many professional gardeners who have neither common sense nor skill in the use of the knife; and on the other hand there are amateurs, careful and observant men, who are competent to undertake the work.

We are assuming that pruning is necessary, as the opponents of the practice have not as yet made out a sufficiently good case to warrant practical men in adopting their views. Pruning, if unnatural, is more than useless ; it is positively injurious. Good pruning is work done in harmony with the wants and peculiarities of each tree, and is to that extent natural. Taking again the rose as an illustration, the free-flowering teas and Bourbons may be pruned often and freely, for as fast as they can be induced to make wood they show flower-buds, but if hybrid perpetuals are similarly treated they simply make wood; a few of the freest bloomers among them will blossom in any case, but the shyest will seldom, if ever, flower. Even skilled and careful gardeners cannot prune every rose in exact accordance with its habits and nature, because each differs in some particulars, and needs to be made a special study of to be properly understood and mastered. But there are leading principles which may be applied, and in few words these are—to prune the freest blooming varieties of rose the hardest, and the shyest bloomers as cautiously and as little as possible. In all cases strong young wood should be left on the plant in preference to weakly and old; and as far as possible all old, misplaced, and spent shoots should be cut out, leaving no sign of a stump to show or to foster disease and blight.

With reference to the pruning of fruit trees, there is the same necessity for care and caution, and an intimate acquaintance with the wants and peculiarities of each tree, as with roses. In no case can pruning be done to advantage at haphazard. There is quite enough in the subject to occupy one man's time and study if it were a work always requiring to be done. But it is not, and hence we have no professional pruners, men who have mastered this branch of gardening alone. The peach tree stands in need of heavier pruning than it usually receives in Queensland to enable it to do its best. The wood to *leave on* is the *strong shoots of the previous season's growth*, on which at *every joint* will be seen *the blossom buds in pairs* with a leaf-bud between them. First, all small weakly wood, and all shoots which cross each other, must be cut clean out, until all the wood on the tree is evenly placed and all fairly strong. Then the leading shoots should be shortened back moderately until the amount of blossom left is ample to produce a fair crop. The pruning should be done with an eye to keep the top of the tree open, and to make the lower branches spread over the ground to shade it.

To speak a little more particularly on this matter, a well-pruned tree should have its leading branches extending gradually outwards and upwards from the stem ; and with many kinds of fruit trees these should be furnished with smaller fruiting branchlets or spurs, thickly studded round the previous year's growth. The apple, pear, plum, apricot, and cherry bear thus and require to be pruned accordingly. When young trees are allowed to grow unpruned the lower portions of the branches are invariably found bare, and the fruit is borne along the upper portions of the shoots, where they are exposed to winds and the scorching sun, and the tree quickly loses its balance. This is of frequent occurrence in Queensland, and hence the straggling and unsightly growths which meet the eye in our colonial orchards. A little care during the first few years in the matter of pruning will go far towards rendering cutting in after years almost, if not altogether, unnecessary. In all pruning, every cut made should have an obvious meaning; and the following illustrations and observations, if attended to, will convey to the new beginner what may be regarded as the first principles of the art. In the illustration, the first line, marked *a*, illustrates a cut made *too far above* a bud, and the effect on the shoot would be that the piece of wood above the bud would die back, and probably carry death with it all down the shoot. Another extreme must also be avoided, as illustrated by the acutely oblique line *c*, which shows a cut *too close* to the bud, leaving only a mere slip of wood to support it, with the bud exposed on every point of the shoot, so that the slightest accident would be apt to destroy it. The line *b* shows exactly the direction and position a cut should take in pruning, the wound being so placed that it will be quickly surrounded by the new growth of the following year. This point being settled, it is next important to know at which bud the knife should be used, and the following sketch will help our readers in their selection.

Fig. 1. represents the head of a young two-year-old tree well filled with buds. The object of pruning being to extend the tree outwards to let the light and air into the centre of the tree, selection must be made accord-

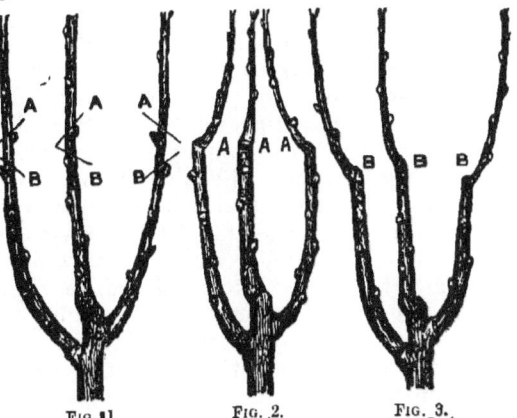

Fig. 1.   Fig. 2.   Fig. 3.

ingly. To do this a spot on each of the branches just above the buds *pointing outwards*, as the letters B B B, must be selected. This will produce the effect shown as in Fig. 3, the branches starting from the terminal buds all pointing outwards. Had the cuts been made at A A A, or near buds *pointing inwards*, the result would have been the shoots would have turned inwards as in Fig. 2, throwing the tree out of shape and spoiling it for fruiting purposes. The entire art and mystery of pruning is shown in the simple rules and illustrations furnished, subject always to such modifications as may meet the special requirements of any particular tree.

Apple and pear trees ought to be pruned cautiously, especially while young. The pear is best encouraged to take a pyramidal form, and should therefore be trained to grow in a single perpendicular stem, with branches forming laterally on all sides equally. No shortening back is necessary, but simply the cutting clean away of any weak or misplaced shoots. The apple requires different treatment. Like the peach, it should be *pruned to an open centre*, and so as to induce the *outer branches* to spread *horizontally*. Pomologists affirm that horizontal wood is more to be depended upon to bear fruit than vertical, and therefore apple trees need encouragement to induce them to make wood most likely to bear fruit. *Apple* branches ought to be shortened back only moderately in any case, and not at all unless straggling. All weakly, watery, or misplaced shoots must be cut away.

In pruning plums let it be borne in mind that the fruit requires plenty of shade, and a spreading habit will best furnish that. The fruit is borne on short spurs along the branches, and weak laterals may be cut clean away, and all crowded or crossed wood where chafing would be likely to result. While shortening back long straggling points of branches, the operator should avoid as far as possible giving the finished tree the appearance of having been clipped with a pair of shears.

The pruning of evergreens is another matter. A moderate thinning all over is best for them, and nowhere should any wood or stems be laid bare. Of course, in all pruning the balance of the tree should be studied; for that helps a tree very much to withstand the effects of rude blasts and rough storms. Symmetry must also be taken into the account, as well as the general balance. The results of good pruning are more certain crops of finer fruits, and greater vigour and endurance to the tree, with much greater symmetry and general attractiveness in every respect. Even conifers and ornamental shrubs and trees are improved in appearance by timely and judicious pruning.

Tall standards should be in every case avoided in this colony. They enable the wind to have too much of its own way with the trees, and they give the sun too much chance of pouring its fervid rays upon the surface of the ground; and dwarfing the trees prevents this. In colder countries with a more regular rainfall the conditions are in every way so different that but little comparison can be fairly drawn between them. Treatment exceedingly suitable and in every way satisfactory may be adopted in the one case which would be entirely unsuited in the other. The art of gardening in Queensland in many of its branches is very distinct from the same in the temperate clime of England; and to be successful in the treatment of many plants and fruits here calls for a fair share of common sense in adapting one's self and one's labour to very altered circumstances of climate, sunshine, and rainfall.

RECEIPT FOR GRAFTING-WAX.

Grafting-wax is very much used on the Continent for protecting newly-made grafts instead of the clay and horse droppings formed into a plaster, such as is commonly used. It is also of great service in covering fresh wounds in trees, made either by accident or design, and is a much more cleanly substance, as well as a more neat application, than the ordinary grafting-clay.

The form here given has borne the test of experience:—

Black pitch	4 parts
Rosin	4 parts
Yellow wax	2 parts
Tallow	1 part

It requires to be melted in an earthen pot over a fire, and *to be applied warm*, but not so hot as to injure the tissue of the bark with which it may come into contact.

BUSH-HOUSES.

To many in Queensland the term "bush-house," so often used in works on gardening and horticultural journals, is unintelligible. Not having seen such a structure, and being anything but familiar with its advantages, all that they read about them is puzzling and obscure. Being quite certain that these structures are destined to play a very important part in our Queensland gardening, and increasingly so as they are better known, some attempt is made in this short article to make the matter more intelligible, so as to enable the general reader to set to work and construct one for himself.

The term "shade-house" is preferred by some, and shade is undoubtedly the essential idea in a bush-house; but there is shade and shade. That is to say there is shade that is favourable to plant life, and there is shade more or less death-dealing towards it. To know the one from the other, and to act accordingly, is the great thing in forming these structures. In constructing a bush-house the object aimed at is to break the rays of a fervid sun, and at the same time moderate the temperature. The idea that naturally occurs to the amateur gardener is to furnish shade by means of living plants, such as evergreen climbers trained over a framework of any required dimensions. Experience has shown this to be a shade that kills, by weakening the nurslings under it, and unfitting them in consequence to properly fulfil their functions. Science steps in to explain the matter by showing that the rays of light are filtered through the living foliage and thereby deprived of life-giving qualities, so that plants struggling under it are thereby robbed of what is necessary to invigorate and strengthen them, and they become failures. Under a shade of dead boughs widely different results are obtained. While the boughs break the sun's rays and thereby reduce the temperature and evaporation to a minimum, light, charged with vitalising and invigorating powers, is shed upon the plants grown under such shade, and, if at all adapted to the climate in which they are grown, they thrive admirably, and give, in many instances, unbounded satisfaction. An error in this is more or less fatal, owing to the cause mentioned; but apart from that objection, a living shade is not sufficiently under control to meet with approval from an expert. It will, at times, grow much too thick, and effectually exclude the light, and it is not possible to regulate such shade so as to suit the requirements of plants growing beneath it. It will be seen therefore that the only shade admissible for securing health and vigour in plants growing under it, is such as dead boughs or dead timber in some form can furnish.

Bush or shade houses are useful for growing ferns, orchids, and many tender and beautiful plants and shrubs, and may be made of any height or dimensions, and in any form or fashion that taste and fancy may dictate. Another use to which they may be put, and which will certainly follow when their true value is more widely known, is for the cultivation of salads and tender vegetables which are most appreciated and sought after when they are most difficult to raise—that is, during the heat of summer, the very time when they are most enjoyable and refreshing. It is in the tropics, and where the heat is steady and constant, they will prove of most service. Plants belonging to cooler climes, such as lettuce, celery, and other salads, and the deservedly popular rhubarb and other things which will suggest themselves to the practical mind, can be raised fit for use in a bush-house in a climate or season when they would not have a show in the open ground. In short, the bush-house can be made to serve a purpose the very reverse of the hothouses and conservatories of cooler climes, by moderating the temperature and maintaining a fairly moist atmosphere —two essentials to the successful growth of many deservedly popular ornamental and useful plants.

What can surpass in attractiveness a well-ordered and select fernery? Anyone with an eye to the beautiful can appreciate such an addition to the well-furnished home. A bush-house provides the necessary shelter for these gems of vegetation, and by procuring a few dray-loads of vegetable mould or peaty soil and investing in choice specimens of these charming and widely differing plants any amount of attractiveness and pleasure may be secured, and at a comparatively very trifling cost. In order that the fernery may answer for some of the choicer varieties the walls of the building should be close to exclude cold and cutting winds, but if only hardy kinds are employed the walls need be no closer than the roof. For orchids the walls must be close, and in the far north of Queensland the possibilities in orchid culture are great, and if followed up with taste and enthusiasm will furnish unlimited enjoyment and satisfaction. For salads, &c., shade to subdue the heat and conserve moisture is all that is necessary, and much less costly structures than are in constant use in the old country for raising tender plants—such as glass-houses and frames—will suffice for the purpose.

Dimensions will be necessarily governed by requirements. A bush-house to grace the surroundings of a well-kept estate and a palatial mansion can be made in keeping therewith; but a bush-house wherein all that is useful and enjoyable may be grown need not be at all costly. Stout uprights of round timber may be let into the ground to support the wall-plates, and the roof may be either flat or have a pitch as fancy may dictate. For the rest there must be a sufficient number of cross-pieces, rafters, or whatever they may be termed, to carry the brush, and when the brush is laid on a few wires drawn lengthwise over them, and secured to the main timber of the building to keep them from shifting, and that will furnish as serviceable quarters for plants as a more costly structure. The height of the roof must depend upon the plants intended to be grown therein. If for ferns or orchids the wall should be sufficiently high to allow the uprights to carry stag's horn, elk's horn, and bird's nest ferns, and to give space for growing epiphytal ferns, lycopodiums, and so forth, in every available spot where they can add to the general effect. Hollow logs can have ferns, begonias, and similarly suitable plants growing in them; rugged limbs of fantastic shape may have ferns and orchids secured upon them to any required height; and wherever convenient besides hanging baskets or masses of ferns may be suspended from the roof, and by this meams a very pleasing and surprising effect may be produced. Following up the idea further, any wall of the fernery may be packed with peat between two walls, the outermost of wood and the inner of wire netting; and then the whole of the wall may be planted with ferns, orchids, and other suitable plants, and in that way be made immensely attractive. When plants are elevated thus of course a syringe will be necessary to give the necessary water, and help them to maintain their vigour. For salads and vegetables a wall sufficiently high to allow free passage through it without stooping will suffice, and the borders underneath will only require to be dealt with as in the usual way in the open ground. The borders in a fernery may be built with rocks or shells and suitable soil, according to any arrangement or device that fancy may dictate; and the nearer the approach in appearance to rude nature's wildness the greater will be the charm. By all means have a bush-house if you wish to have a charming retreat in connection with your home; and the probability is when once you have experienced the charm and the advantage of having one, you will aspire to make an extended acquaintance with them.

FLOWER CULTURE.

This is not only a broad and a comprehensive subject, but it is also one of especial interest to all. Well, yes; there are a few who take no interest in any flower but a cauliflower; still as such cases are fortunately only very exceptional, it will be pleasing and profitable to cater for the wants and wishes of the many. Things pleasing to the eye and to gratify the sense of smell, are as necessary contributions towards satisfying human nature as those that satisfy any other requirement. In gratifying the sense of vision and in surrounding ourselves with fragrance by the cultivation of flowers we, at the same time, furnish nature with a laboratory wherein by chemical aid she may manufacture life-giving ozone; and the plants themselves which perform for us this great work, may at the same time be employed in transforming death-dealing decomposing materials into life-giving ones. Beautiful flowers serve other purposes than merely to please the eye and awaken the sense of smell; they have to do with our health and our life, and while doing so they tend to elevate and refine our tastes and our thoughts. It requires a certain amount of taste and refinement to attempt floriculture; but whoever attempts it will certainly strengthen and develop those elevating sentiments, and many other useful qualities besides.

In many particulars floriculture is worked on the same lines as horticulture generally. The same rules, the same laws, and consequently the same treatment is to be applied to the preparation of the soil and such like matters, as are used in growing fruit or vegetables. One point of difference may be singled out, and that is seeing that success in floriculture depends largely upon the growth of annuals, the surface soil of the borders must in all cases be made into a good seed-bed. Trenching, draining, and manuring are indispensable for the growth of good flowers; and the borders for 3 or 4 feet from the path must in every case be such as will promote the successful germination of the seeds of choice annuals. Another item will help in that direction, and that is keeping the surface soil enriched with leaf-mould or well-rotted manure, for nothing tends more certainly to make a good seed-bed than such treatment.

But the great secret of success in floriculture is a masterful knowledge of the seasons. Seasonable work in every respect is the only reliable way to master the art of horticulture. Some seeds will only germinate when the soil heat is low; others require a tropical heat to start them. To succeed with the former it is either necessary to wait for cold weather to sow seeds in the open ground or to make a degree of artificial coolness with shade of some kind, while to grow the tropical annuals summer heat must be utilised. A complete list of those flower seeds which only germinate and grow in cold weather could hardly be made out, but the following are among the most important:—Sweet-peas, mignonette, larkspur, asters, pansies, violets, carnations, picotees, pinks, candytuft, sweet william, hollyhocks, phlox Drummondii, stocks, wallflowers, and many other favourites; for summer sowing we have balsams, cockscombs, zinnia elegans, verbenas, amaranths, petunias, portulaccas, dahlias, and some others. Annuals form the principal attraction in many well-kept gardens, and cannot therefore be profitably neglected. Supposing the right season is chosen to sow the seeds, the next thing to attend to is how to raise them best. Make a bed of some good rich compost in some convenient place and sow the seeds in rows, putting tallies to them with name of plant and date of sowing thereon. See they are shaded and regularly watered; and when large enough to handle transplant them into rich soil, where they are to remain. Put them one in a place, and if you choose group them; and if they have not flowered before you put them out so that you could learn their quality, plant them as thick again as you intend them to remain, so that when they bloom you may weed out all that prove to be indifferent. This is the way to improve the strain of your choice annuals, and all who take any pride in their floral pets should show their ambition in that way. Whether you follow this plan with all flowers or not, be sure and do it with stocks and asters. Stocks are best grouped, a colour in a place; and if seed is wanted from them, leave only one single flower in a patch of many. Treat asters the same, only leaving double flowers for seed. The principle involved in this will bear almost general application amongst choice flowers of all kinds, but more especially annuals.

Next to annuals in importance comes the rose and ornamental and flowering shrubs generally. Seasonable work amongst these is the item of chief importance. For a rose to give satisfaction it must have room for its roots to feed in, and light and air among its branches to ripen its wood. It is only in very exceptional cases that this is seen. Nurserymen who desire to show their roses at their best invariably do it; and so also do those who are ambitious to carry off the prizes offered at shows. In gardens where beds are crowded with small plants of all kinds and an occasional rose amongst them, an odd flower worth looking at may be seen at rare intervals; but such will be the exception and not the rule. Seasonable planting, seasonable pruning, and so forth, are essentials to success with the rose. From March to August is the proper season for planting them, and for the main pruning June or July is the best; and cuttings made from the prunings may then be planted in beds for striking and planting out another season. The freest flowering roses are the tea, noisettes, Bourbons, and some of the hybrid chinas and perpetuals. Some of the teas and noisettes will bear pruning whenever they are at rest and out of bloom, and such treatment hastens them into blossom again. Hybrid perpetuals must only be pruned during the main pruning season, as mentioned above. The planting season for flowering and ornamental shrubs is the same as the rose, and the pruning season is the same.

Seasonable propagation is another item in successful floriculture. Nearly all biennials and perennials have to be renewed at times, and young plants to replace them require to be struck from cuttings. During autumn and winter is the best time to succeed with most cuttings, and the best method is to make shady beds, prepare your cuttings, plant them carefully and closely in rows 1 foot or 15 inches apart and keep the soil moist until signs of growth appear; then with a garden trowel they can be lifted and transplanted anywhere they are required. The saving of seeds and the storing of bulbs are items requiring seasonable attention, but these are matters to be regulated according to circumstances. The few hints given in this short chapter will be very helpful to all who contemplate floriculture.

HINTS ON POULTRY KEEPING.

ALTHOUGH poultry keeping is not gardening, the two should always go hand in hand, for the one may be said to be the complement of the other, whether viewed from the poultry or the human side. Keeping fowls will help to grow the vegetables, and growing vegetables will help to keep the fowls; so it is pretty clear that poultry-keeping is intimately related to gardening. Not that fowls are good gardeners, by any means; but they help good gardeners with a means of cultivating advantageously by the valuable manure they make, if that is only estimated at its correct value, and properly stored and made use of.

But poultry keeping is a comprehensive term and wants defining to be intelligible. The term poultry includes ordinary domestic fowls, ducks, geese, turkeys, pigeons, and guinea fowls. These are not all alike profitable, nor are they at all times equally desirable to keep should our fancy incline us that way. Domestic fowls is the chief concern of ordinary housekeepers, so if attention is concentrated upon these, and useful hints thrown out to assist in their management help will thereby be afforded to the many.

Says one, "Can you recommend me a good breed of fowls for laying eggs? I have been bothered a good deal at different times with various breeds and crosses; but get what I will they furnish me with eggs only when eggs are cheap. When 'eggs are eggs' I look in vain for them." Just so, my friend. Many have found that same rut and could not get out of it. Feeding and shelter have as much to do with that matter as anything else. Unless fowls are properly fed— *i.e.*, sufficiently fed on proper food; and also properly housed and cared for, it matters but little what strain of fowls you get. Not that breed is an unimportant item in itself; still it is far, very far from being everything. We hear a great deal about the "common barn-door fowl" being as useful for all purposes as any. But what is it in the first place; and when that is made out to our satisfaction, where are they to be had? It may be taken for granted that running after high-priced and fancy breeds of fowls is not the way for common people to make fowls profitable. So the "common barn-door fowl" might be right enough if it could be identified; but there is the rub. Every mongrel lot of fowls is thought to be this old fashioned profitable variety; but the fact is it is hard or impossible to define or identify it. In America Plymouth Rocks, Houdans, and Langshans are praised as egg producers. In other parts of the world Black Spanish, Polanders, and the several varieties of the Hamburgs have that character. But from trials made it would appear that climate has to do with the question; for a breed that is thrifty and lays well in a cool climate is not as great a success in a warm one. Queensland testimony is not in favour of the Black Spanish, principally because the climate is found unsuitable. The Polanders are more hardy and lay well, but the eggs are so small as to be objectionable. Judges everywhere are now declaring in favour of the silver-spangled Hamburgs as good layers, and it is more than likely that they will be found to "fill the bill" as well, if not better, than any other variety in this colony, that is as egg-producers. If flesh and size of bird is taken principally into account, there are the several varieties of Brahmapootra and Cochin-china fowls to select from; and taking all things into account, where there is a garden these larger breeds of fowls are safer to keep, as they never fly high and are easily kept from flying the garden fence. It cannot be said that they are good layers, but with proper feeding they are as good winter layers as any, and to lay in winter is to the point, for then it is that " eggs are eggs."

Having decided upon the breed, the next thing is to house them properly; for unless they are properly cared for in this respect they will not prove profitable. "What," says one, "do you mean to say that housing fowls increases their laying powers?" Yes; I say so. "Well, then," says he, "we disagree; for my father kept fowls in Tasmania for years, which roosted every night in some elm trees summer and winter, not being housed at all, and they laid well." That may be. But while fowls may lay well they must be protected from native cats, iguanas, crows, hawks, and snakes; all of which count eggs and chickens their lawful prey, and this proper housing will do. Proper housing will comprehend a sufficient shelter from the fervid rays of the sun; suitable contrivances for watering the birds; good nest accommodation, and a sufficient protection from the raids of their many enemies. These are all things to be provided for by the poultry keeper. It is neither necessary nor desirable that a close house should be built; all that need be close about it is the roof, which should be as good as for a dwelling-house. The remainder must be sufficient to exclude vermin so that eggs and young birds may be secure; but freeness of circulation everywhere is an advantage rather than otherwise, and possibly the best thing to make the sides and ends of a poultry house with is wire netting; fine enough near the ground to keep out their enemies, and coarse everywhere else.

Accommodation for roosting may be furnished in a variety of ways. Roosts in the form of broad ladders are very good, made so that they can be shifted for a systematic cleaning up now and then. The perches should be placed so that fowls may roost high or low according to their nature; and no perch should be exactly over another. Heavy fowls require a perch they can squat down upon, something as broad and flat as a batten or a narrow board, and at the same time strong enough to bear a good weight, so that a batten itself would not do. Drinking water may be furnished variously, but it should always be where it can keep cool and clean, and the supply should always be kept up and as pure as possible. Some give their fowls water in a trough elevated on trussle legs, and the idea is by no means bad, as it tends to keep the water clean by preventing ducks and water birds from puddling and messing it. The same plan is also good for feeding fowls, if the trough be only large enough to accommodate the number. Nothing contributes more directly to keeping fowls in health than cleanliness—clean water, clean food, and clean quarters. Another essential for successful poultry-keeping is a good run for the birds, where they can hunt for insects of all kinds besides getting plenty of green food. It is surprising what a number of grasshoppers and insects of all sorts a healthy fowl will catch and consume; and when there is plenty of grass and green stuff they will put away a large share of that too, and be all the better for it. Food in variety is best for everything. For fowls the staple should be maize, but if it can be supplied in a crushed or mealed state it will serve them much better than if it were whole. Some successful poultry-raisers prefer to feed their fowls on a mixture of flour and bran mixed and wetted. A certain proportion of meat minced and mixed with it is also very good to produce eggs, and if it is occasionally spiced with cayenne mildly it will be helpful.

Conveniences for laying is another important item. A very good plan adopted by some is to fix a number of small boxes on one end of the fowl-house at some distance from the ground where the fowls can lie quiet and be unmolested. There must be a landing in front of each box and a nest inside with a nest-egg, and a dozen of these can easily be arranged in a small space. But where there are many fowls and more laying accommodation is called for, nest boxes may be placed around the yard anywhere so long as the fowls can be in them and protected from the weather; and above all things they like to lay their eggs in some dark, shady and secluded spot. In making laying nests other than those on the walls no bottom is required to the boxes. All that is needful is to excavate a hollow in the ground under the box and put in the nest-egg. The trouble experienced with poultry keeping is doing battle with lice. One very good preventive is a dust-bath. Fowls should have access to loose dry earth or wood-ashes, and then they will enjoy themselves occasionally by wallowing in it, which is a great preventive of this pest. When lice become plentiful vigorous measures require to be taken to get rid of them. One of the best remedies is to paint or otherwise moisten every part or thing pertaining to the fowl-house with kerosene, which will effectually kill every insect it touches. Nests may be kept free of them by dusting them occasionally with Calvert's carbolic powder, or by putting old tobacco leaves about them.

With reference to sitting hens some pains should be taken, and in doing so the first thing necessary is to sit them out of harm's way—that is to say, where snakes and iguanas cannot molest them. It is often said that fowls making their own nests succeed best in bringing out their chicks; so they do, provided no enemy discovers them, but that is frequently the case. Hens generally strive to isolate themselves when sitting, and this should be attended to by the poultry keeper, or she will be often disturbed by other hens coming to the nest, which may drop additional eggs into the nest unnoticed, to be addled and wasted. Isolate your sitting hens, therefore. Boxes of the size requisite for laying hens are as well adapted for sitting them. These boxes should have no bottom, and the eggs to be hatched are best laid in a hollow made in the earth itself, which, if a little moist, will be an advantage. The top should be a hinged lid, and one side—intended for the hen's ingress and egress—should be made to slide in and out, so as to shut the hen in entirely while sitting, only making such provision as is necessary for ventilation. Outside of the box should be a small run shut in with wire netting, and inside this should be a dust bath, a supply of water, and when the hen is let out daily, a supply of food should be put in. While the hen is feeding see that the eggs are all right, and from time to time dust them with carbolic powder, or ashes and sulphur mixed, to keep down lice. If the weather is warm there is no necessity for hurrying the hen back to her eggs, for half-an-hour or an hour is not sufficient to do them any injury in such case. Warm nests are a mistake in this climate, but are right enough for America or suchlike cold countries. Keep correct account of the date of sitting, and of the time when they should come out. It is always well to sit two or more hens at the same time, or near about it, so that if the hatching be a partial failure, the chicks may all be put with one mother, for it is very wasteful to see a hen running for months with only two or three chicks. Or after the two have sat a week you may find out how many are fertile; and if anything like a large proportion are likely to miss, the two lots may be put under one hen, and a fresh lot substituted for the other. While the hens are sitting it is a good plan to occasionally sprinkle the nest and eggs with water, and especially when they are nearing the time for coming out; for want of this the chicks are often unable to break their way out.

When the chicks are out suitable food must be provided for them. The best is hard-boiled eggs chopped and crumbled up small and mixed with maize or oatmeal. Stop the eggs after a day or two and give the meal alone mixed with bread crumbs or boiled potatoes—sweet or otherwise—and kitchen scraps. Do not give them wet or sloppy food, and let them be where they can pick up small stones or gravel to aid digestion. Keep them well supplied with clear water, and shade and protect them for a few days under a coop from hawks and other enemies, and by the time they are ten days or a fortnight old they may be allowed to run at large. Where chickens are raised for sale it is best to have a yard for them to run in away from other fowls; and for every hen to be separated from the rest as they are extremely liable to inflict injury if not kill the chicks belonging to another brood. In conclusion, it may be as well to say that in every industry those who pay the best attention to it are the most successful, and it will never pay to keep fowls unless they are well cared and provided for and well tended.

FIELD AND GARDEN CALENDAR.

JANUARY.

IN THE FIELD the work of harvesting the wheat crop is about over and the plough should be put in the land the first opportunity afterwards. Maize for a late crop may still be sown, but to make sure of ripening it would be advisable to put in only early maturing varieties. It may not be generally known that moderately thick planting serves to expedite the period of maturity, so that, although thick sowing may generally not be advisable, to hasten the ripening of a late crop it would be as well to adopt it. The planting of sweet potatoes will now need to be pushed forward vigorously to ensure a crop before the frosts of winter set in. To prevent failure when planting the cuttings about a pint of water should be given to each, even if the soil be tolerably moist, so as to settle the earth well about them and give them a chance of a fair and even start. The planting of sugar-cane may be continued with good chances of success; indeed, it is fast becoming the opinion in Queensland that from January to April is about the very best season in the year to plant out. In the southern districts, however, or anywhere that frost is severe, it is now late. Rice sowing may now be done, for with abundance of moisture there is yet time for the grain to mature, and our small selectors will probably find it to their advantage to grow rice rather than maize. Tropical fodder plants, such as millet, sorghum, imphee, and téosinte may still be sown, but unless the last-named is put into rich and well-prepared land, the chances of a profitable crop will be doubtful. Téosinte requires a continuous high temperature and no frost, to show itself to advantage; but, when it succeeds, it yields large quantities of a very excellent fodder. It is only suitable, therefore, for the Central and Northern districts. Late in the month a small sowing of mangel-wurzel may be made, but the full crop would be better if delayed another month or six weeks, as when put in too early it falls a prey to the fly and its larvæ. At the end of the month, also, a good sowing of cabbage of some large-growing variety, such as the drumhead or Schweinfurt, may be made, to be transplanted later on for stock-feeding purposes. Nothing is better suited as feed for milch cows than the cabbage, and our dairymen should therefore take the hint and provide themselves with a full supply. As a stand-by for stock-feeding hardly anything surpasses the pumpkin, and not to be too late, seed should be sown with as little delay as possible. Look well after the tobacco crop, and make a point of choosing a dry interval for gathering it and hanging it in the drying shed. Follow up weeds with persistency and determination, as it is either you or they for it; and, after all, timely cleaning operations are the most profitable of all the work done upon the farm.

In the KITCHEN GARDEN, preparations should now be made for a full supply of vegetables for winter and spring use. Choose a shady border and moist weather for sowing cabbage and cauliflower seeds, and do not neglect to lightly tread the seed in and mulch it after sowing. Avoid growing or living shade for seed-beds. All shade for important seed-beds should be artificial, as living shade robs the young plants of the food and moisture provided for them. Continue to sow French beans at intervals of two or three weeks. Radishes and lettuces may be sown in rich and well-prepared soil in all the cooler parts of the colony. Prepare a bed of rich earth in as shady a place as possible for sowing celery. Being an aquatic plant plenty of moisture should be supplied, and a thin mulch used to prevent the surface soil from becoming dry. Transplant eschalots in favourable weather. Manure and trench all vacant plots for a full sowing of peas, beans, carrots, parsnips, and root crops generally, and for a first planting of cabbage and cauliflower plants during February. Continue to sow sweet or white corn at intervals, also the long runner bean and spinach. Keep all clean.

In the FRUIT department, keep a watchful eye on all recently-planted trees to see that they are not suffering at all from drought or other causes. Continue to thin late varieties of the peach, and bud young stock required for planting out. Look after the grape crop, thinning the bunches where necessary, and guarding them from the depredations of birds and insects by snares and scarecrows, and from the inroads of oidium by the application of sulphur. Keep strawberry beds mulched, as it tends to lower the temperature of the soil—a condition favourable to a plant indigenous to temperate climes. Allow as many runners to grow as are required for planting out in March, and persistently clear away the rest. Make plantations of pine-apples, allowing them ample space for full developement, and keep the land always in a good state of cultivation between the rows. It is almost too late to transplant bananas, except in isolated cases where immunity from frost, or nearly so, can be reckoned upon. Rosellas should have every attention to keep them growing vigorously. Heavily-bearing orange and lemon trees should be well cared for, mulched if dry weather continues, and supplied with a good dressing of liquid manure occasionally; if possible also choosing showery weather for its application, as falling rain will then help very considerably to distribute it thoroughly amongst the feeding rootlets.

In the FLOWER GARDEN now a revival of activity may be anticipated with the more plenteous rainfall of the season. Borders should be lightly dug and manure turned in; all spent and straggling plants of annuals should be removed or cut back; and during showery weather bedding plants of coleus, verbenas, petunias, pelargoniums, heliotropes, and lobelias should be planted out, taking the precaution to shade them with a few boughs until they have begun to start into growth. Roses will now make a fresh growth, and in many cases the judicious use of the knife amongst them in shortening back only the spent and straggling branches, and in cutting clean out all such as have lost their vigour, will tend to promote a profusion of bloom again. These remarks apply particularly to the hybrid China roses, not to the hybrid perpetuals. Secure all tender plants against strong winds; dahlias especially are extremely liable to be mutilated if not properly staked. Budding operations will now require attention; roses in particular should not be neglected longer, and the budding will be the safest if the shady side of the stem is used for inserting the bud.

In the BUSH-HOUSE, see that your shade is good—that is, sufficient to break the rays of the sun without unnecessarily cutting off a full supply of light. Too dense a shade for many things is worse than none. Many of the plants grown under glass will attain to average perfection under shade if properly cared for. Ferns and lycopods are an exception to the rule in the matter of shade, for they mostly love it, and luxuriate most where they have it most perfect; still, without light and circulation of air they cannot mature properly or become hardy. Crotons, coleus, dracenas, caladiums, and other beautiful foliaged plants show themselves to a great advantage in the bush-house, and repay for any extra attention they may receive in watering, shading, and liquid manuring. Endeavour to strike young plants of choice fuchsias to replace older plants, as they speedily become worn out in this climate, and often succumb to continued heat and drought. Gloxinias, achimenes, and other flowering bulbs should now be advancing well into bloom, and would be benefited by a little weak liquid manure occasionally. Cyclamens which have passed blooming may be gradually dried off and put on one side to rest. Keep cinerarias and calceolarias in a cool airy place and moderately dry. See that the water you use is of the same temperature as the air of the shed, and make provision for a proper supply by keeping a tank full exposed to the atmosphere under the shed.

FEBRUARY.

In the FIELD, an effort may yet be made in most of the coast districts to secure a crop of maize. An early maturing variety will be the safest for this season of the year, and those who take the best pains and care to get it in properly will be the most likely to reap advantageously. The latter end of this month is the best for a full crop of maize everywhere North. In all cultivation it is being shown most conclusively that the amount of crop is largely dependent upon the quality and quantity of labour bestowed upon the soil. Those intending to sow lucerne should have their land in readiness by the end of the month, and a fortnight or so later it should be sown. Lucerne is very much benefited by letting the land intended for its reception lie a while after being thoroughly prepared for it, to give weeds an opportunity to start into growth. The scarifier should then be set to work, and the land well cleaned; the seed may be sown afterwards with much better prospects of success. As mentioned in last month, cuttings of sugar-cane may still be planted out. It is well in planting at this season of the year to be particularly careful to have it well under the soil, so that frost may not reach the roots and injure them. If the roots keep right they will start early into growth in the spring as a rattoon crop, and be stronger at the year's end than if put in during September, October, or November. Towards the end of the month land should be in readiness for the reception of swede turnips, mangel-wurzel, carrots, cabbages, and the like, for providing food for stock later in the winter and early spring. Pumpkins may still be sown for the same purpose—more particularly in the tropics. On the principle that better crops are obtained when land is ploughed and left a while to fallow than when ploughed and immediately sown, it is advisable to get the land in readiness for sowing winter oats and barley for fodder purposes. Sorghum and imphee may still be sown, as they are moderately hardy and can withstand several degrees of frost without injury. Téosinte and guinea-grass would not be profitable if sown now—except far north—as they are too decidedly tropical. While the land is dry is the time to haul manure of any kind upon it, and as soon as it is spread it should be ploughed under, or its virtue will in a great degree vanish. A dry time is also the best for cleaning operations, and may in many ways be turned to good account by the practical and industrious farmer. During the month a few English potatoes may be planted, and preference should be given to whole sets rather than cut ones for putting in now. In sheltered localities in the Central, and anywhere in the Northern districts, it is not too late to plant sweet potatoes, but no delay should take place in getting them in as early as possible. Tares or vetches and Cape barley are also crops suitable for sowing this month in the cooler districts.

In the KITCHEN GARDEN, active preparations should be made for getting in a full supply of winter vegetables of all kinds. The preparations necessary in order to secure good results are to stir the soil up to a good depth, and bury a liberal allowance of some good fertiliser therein. The best way to grow good vegetables is to devote a plot of land to them exclusively, and not allow tree or shrub of any kind near. It is then, comparatively speaking, quite an easy matter to trench the land occasionally, and such treatment immensely enriches and improves the texture of the soil. Market gardening, to be really profitable, requires to be carried out on such principles and treatment. Prepare a bed of rich soil where artificial shade can be provided, and sow seeds of cabbage, cauliflower, and celery. To be successful the surface soil must be thoroughly enriched and pulverised; then sow the seeds broadcast upon the surface, and with the back of the spade or with the foot "firm" the seeds in the ground. If the weather is dry give them at once a thorough soaking, and afterwards a light coating of mulch. Take care that the surface never becomes dry, and you will quickly have strong plants. With reference to celery particular attention must be paid to it or it cannot thrive. Sow Tuscarora or some white variety of maize for cooking in the cob, and do it as early in the month as possible or it will stand a poor chance. Sow French beans, giving them from 2 feet to 2 feet 6 inches between the rows, and from 4 inches to 6 inches from plant to plant. Late in the month peas and broad beans may be sown, and a full crop of radishes, lettuces, and watercresses. Anyone having the water laid on could easily grow watercresses. To do so make a trench two feet wide and one foot deep from east to west, and on the north side provide upright artificial shade. Then at the bottom of the trench put six inches of rich compost, and sow the seeds on top, watering them well and keeping them always wet. In this way it is possible to grow watercress anywhere in Queensland. English potatoes should be planted, choosing only whole sets, towards the end of the month. Sweet potatoes may still be planted with a fair chance of success, at any rate in localities not liable to early frosts. Carrots, parsnips, beetroot, salsify, and onions, may also be sow late in the month, and, after sowing and firming them in the ground with the foot, a light mulch should be applied over the surface. As soon as any crop is spent, remove the rubbish and break up the soil, if necessary, adding a good coat of manure to it before digging it. Keep all parts of the garden scrupulously clean, and between all growing crops see that the surface soil is always loose and open. A loose surface soil is a very good mulch, and is a preventive against evaporation.

In the FRUIT GARDEN, it is time to commence operations for intended autumn planting. Trees should never be planted in soil newly broken up and imperfectly tilled; a large proportion of the failures met with in making an orchard is distinctly traceable to such mistakes. As a rule, land intended for fruit trees should be trenched from 18 inches to 30 inches deep. Poor ridgy stony land will carry trees and produce good fruit if the soil is trenched. But be sure that you drain deeper than you trench or your land will prove a grave both to your trees and your hopes. Look well after heavily-bearing trees, and see that the soil is loose and open everywhere about them, and should the weather continue dry apply a good thick coating of mulch all over the roots. Newly planted, tender trees, such as mangoes, custard apples, and tropical fruits of all sorts, will require special attention to encourage them to make a strong start and establish themselves, and then they will have strength for standing better against the cold of winter. Keep the land between the rows of rosellas clean and open by forking the surface or hoeing, and the same with pine-apple plantations and bananas. Gather all fruit as it ripens, and if it is intended for market forward it without delay; or, if it can be kept, store it in as dry and cool a place as you can find. Land intended for vines should be trenched and thoroughly prepared now for planting in spring; a few months fallow for the land allotted to them will make all the difference in their growth when put out. Vines which have not matured their fruit crop from any unusual cause would, in many instances, bear a fair crop yet if some of the leading shoots were cut back. At any rate, the Isabella will bear such treatment.—Large vines desirable to propagate layer as early in the month as possible.

In the FLOWER GARDEN, spare no trouble to get your ground in readiness for the seeds of spring flowering annuals. It is not enough that you tickle the surface with the hoe; you must dig deep and manure well to produce good and abundant bloom, and with proper treatment it is astonishing the amount of flowers even a small garden plot may be made to produce. Nearly any variety of English annuals may be sown towards the end of the month, but it would be necessary to tread in the seeds gently with the foot, and mulch and water them—that is, if the weather is dry—to give them a fair chance to germinate. Balsams and cockscombs would succeed admirably now in suitable soil, the weather being favourable. Roses out of bloom having straggling branches should be pruned lightly to encourage them to grow and flower. All vacancies in the borders should be filled in moist weather with bedding plants of favourite kinds, such as verbenas, petunias, geraniums, penstemons, and—in some situations—with fuchsias, but these last would need to be shaded while the heat lasted, and in the cold weather of our winter they would luxuriate. Study cleanliness and arrangement without any intermission.

The BUSH-HOUSE will need attention in hot dry weather, and it will also well repay it. Of course the plants favoured with such shelter are largely grown in pots, and must have a due share of attention even to live, and a little more than that to make them vigorous and thrifty. Beware of having such places under living trees of any kind. In many instances strong-growing trees appropriate to themselves the lion's share of the food and moisture you are applying to your favourites, and they (the trees) flourish while your pets are starved or suffer a lingering death. Even when over-shadowing trees do not injure in that way they do so in others, and consequently the only course to follow with a bush-house is never to have it in the vicinity of any large trees. Now is the time to strike cuttings of coleus and crotons; a moist bottom heat and a close frame are the greatest essentials to successful propagation in these matters. Strike cuttings of fuchsias, geraniums, double-petunias, and begonias; and if a few bulbs of ranunculus and anemone were potted towards the end of the month they would show to pretty good advantage in such a situation. Regulate the shade carefully at all times, so that it shall neither be too dense nor too open.

MARCH.

In the FIELD, fodder crops of various kinds should be sown: oats and barley are the principal favourites, but there are farmers scattered here and there who have a preference for wheat, even for making into hay, principally because it will yield a heavier return in suitable soils during dry weather. Be that as it may, a full sowing of some good fodder should now be made. Lucerne can also be sown to advantage in the fall, always supposing the land is thoroughly clean where it is sown. Sowing in drills is best, and the drills should not be closer than 15 inches, although the usual practice is to make them only 6 inches apart. The reason for sowing in drills is to facilitate cultivation between the rows while the plants are small and at times when the lucerne is cut, but unless 15 inches clear space is left between each row this cannot be, and drilling has little or no advantage over broadcast sowing in that case. If it is thought that by sowing thick a greater weight per acre will be realised it is simply a mistake, for the reverse is the experience of all who have tried it: and, moreover, the wider the space left between the rows the longer will it keep producing during a dry spell. To sow an acre 14 lbs. of seed should suffice if properly drilled in, while 20 lbs. is none too much when sown broadcast. Swede turnips, mangel-wurzel, kohl rabi, and carrots may all be sown now in deeply worked land in a good state of fertility. Unless the land is quite rich none of these crops will pay, and possibly no manure can be had that will give better returns than superphosphate of lime or bone dust. This manure is exceedingly portable and a few hundredweight of it will go a long way. For feeding stock, together with root crops, cabbage could be grown now, and it possesses this advantage over many others, that it can remain in the field until cut for use. Cabbages unmixed are not good food for milch cows, as they make the milk strong in flavour; mangel-wurzel and carrots are among the best feeding roots for milch kine. Forward crops of maize should be attended to, harvesting them as soon as ripe. Sorghum, imphee, and maize for fodder purposes may still be sown. Land intended for wheat should now be ploughed deep and left in the rough to mellow. It is almost too late for planting sugar-cane, except in very sheltered localities and out of the way of frost, but where drought has prevented its being got in sooner a little may be tried, taking the precaution to cover it sufficiently from chilling winds.

In the KITCHEN GARDEN, make an effort to get in a full crop of vegetables of nearly all kinds. Sow cabbage and cauliflower seeds in well-prepared and thoroughly-enriched beds. If plants are procurable they are much to be preferred, and should be planted out at once in land thoroughly enriched, deeply worked, and well pulverised. In poor land plant them close, for they cannot make much growth so as to occupy it otherwise; but in land rich and deep beware of putting them too close, as the crop will suffer. Sow peas and broad-beans, and by putting in early and late varieties of the former at one sowing you will provide for a succession. Both these vegetables require the land to be in good heart, and they show more vigour and productiveness in strong soils. Sow French beans also in rich soil; in another month it will be getting late for them, except far north, where the winter, if moist, is best for them. Carrots, parsnips, and beet should all be sown now, and if sown in drills and mulched until above the ground it will be of great assistance. Sow salads of all kinds, not forgetting watercress. If obtainable, cuttings of the latter are preferable to seed, and should be pricked out in the prepared soil and well watered. Finish by making a shade of boughs or such like on the sunny side and partly over the top, to exclude the sun's rays and allow the entrance of light. A good watering twice a week, or oftener, afterwards will bring them on well. Swede and other turnips should now be sown, and a sprinkle of superphosphate of lime sown with the seed is found very helpful to check the ravages of the turnip-fly. Divide and plant sage, thyme, marjoram, and pot herbs of all kinds, and sow seeds of the same; also, make a good sowing of parsley. Make free use of water with all growing vegetables as far as possible, and when plants are strong and appear to need assistance apply weak liquid manure carefully to the roots; the latter is best done in wet weather, or at least before a shower. Asparagus beds should be prepared now, and the seeds sown soon after. Thoroughly trench and manure a strip—say 3 feet wide and 15 feet long—fully 2 feet deep, and divide the surface into three drills, the outer two about 9 inches from the edge of the bed, and the third in the middle. In these sow your seed thinly, and when they come up thin them out, leaving the strongest plants from 12 inches to 15 inches asunder in the rows. Prepare land similarly for rhubarb, and sow seed or plant roots, as may be most desirable. Plant celery in rich moist land, and push it on by copious and frequent waterings, for, being an aquatic plant, it cannot live in a dry situation. With reference to earthing, leave it altogether undone until it has made its full growth; then earth and blanch it, and you will have a more solid celery than by earthing it from the first. Divide and plant potato onions, and sow onion seed in well-enriched land. Night-soil serves admirably for onions.

In the FRUIT GARDEN, set to work preparing land for the reception of trees. This is a work that should never be left to do when the trees are ready to go in, but should always be done in time to allow the air to penetrate the soil and fit it for the proper reception of the roots. Neglect of this is the cause of losses every season. Trench, drain, and manure all orchard plots. No one should think of putting in a tree unless all these operations are duly attended to, for when neglected the tree has no chance to yield a return, and what can be a fitting return for neglect? Gather all fruit as it ripens, and carefully store in a cool, airy, and dry place, or market it. Look for the first appearance of blight or disease in your trees, and, as far as possible, study to ascertain the cause. It may be that the soil is too wet, or blight may be sapping their vitals, or the trees may be growing on an unsuitable stock. If the first is the case, drain, and do it at once; if the second, apply a wash of soft soap, sulphur, and chloride of lime, by means of a syringe, over every portion of the plant; if the latter, root it out and replace it with something better, for an unsuitable stock is an everlasting mistake and cannot be corrected in any other way. Layer vines which it is desirable to propagate, and set to work at once trenching and breaking up new land intended for vine culture. Keep land thoroughly clean and free from undergrowth in the vicinity of trees; a good coating of mulch to heavily-bearing trees is always an advantage, for, while keeping the roots cool and moist, it provides a clean bed for ripe fruit to fall upon.

In the FLOWER GARDEN, the utmost activity should be manifested in preparing the borders for the seeds of English annuals, which should be sown at once, and for trenching and manuring where roses and choice shrubs are intended to be planted. Whatever you do, see that all your flower beds are kept in good heart with manure and thoroughly clean ; then your land may be expected to do its best. In showery weather fill up all the vacancies with bedding plants of various kinds, and carefully sow seeds of pansies and English double daisies. Make and renew borders of alternantheras or any other ornamental edging preferred. Plant bulbs of gladiolus and all spring flowering varieties ; bulbs grown in the southern colonies should have the preference. Plant roses in showery weather, and rooted layers of pinks, carnations, and picotees. Roses may yet be budded with a fair chance of success if good stocks are ready to take them. Tie up and stake chrysanthemums, trim edgings, and keep all snug and tidy.

In the BUSH-HOUSE, a good deal of useful work may now be done in propagating. Cuttings of coleus, crotons, fuchsias, geraniums, heliotropes, and hosts of things besides, may now be struck. Seeds of cineraria, calceolaria, and China primula, may be sown in pots filled with rich mellow compost. Sow them on the surface, firm them in, and water them with a fine rose; then cover each pot with glass to preserve the surface moisture. Repot fuchsias into a lively compost, and start them into active growth. Add to your fernery with choice varieties, and keep all clean. Beware of the tendency to overcrowd, for it will effectually bar success.

APRIL.

In the FIELD, an early sowing of wheat is now considered absolutely necessary in order to escape from rust, and all wheat-growers should always run the broad-tinted cultivator over the stubble field immediately after the crop is reaped ; the ground being then soft, a large area is quickly gone over, and the advantage is most apparent when circumstances allow of ploughing being set about. Although there are very few who now believe that any treatment of the seed-wheat will lessen the damage from rust, there is a growing opinion in the southern colonies that the constant pickling in strong bluestone has really had a deteriorating effect upon the general stamina of the plant. Farmers should try thinner sowing when they are able to get the seed in early ; also they should see if they cannot take a leaf out of Major Hallet's book. Barley and oats can now be sown for hay and seed purposes, or for green food for winter use ; for the latter purpose successional sowings of small plots will be found the most advantageous course to adopt. For winter feed maize can still be sown, but the frost will not allow it to mature seed. Only in a few favoured spots untouched by the winter frosts can potatoes now be depended upon to succeed; wherever any have been put in it is necessary that they should be well cultivated. The few farmers who are again trying cotton-growing must keep a sharp watch to gather the cotton as fast as the bolls expand, before they get injured by rain. Tobacco growers should now also be busy cutting and housing the leaves as they arrive at maturity. This is the month of the year for sowing grasses; on the Downs, particularly, it is necessary to get them in and the plants established before the cold winds of winter. In sowing grasses for permanent pasture in Queensland they should be allowed the whole field to themselves—that is, they should not be sown among cereals. Another thing to be noted is that it does not do to " scamp" them in; to be successful, except in a few naturally well-favoured localities, thorough tillage is absolutely necessary. Lucerne, prairie-grass, vetches, &c., should now be sown; give them also a thoroughly prepared seedbed. Few farmers grow as many turnips and carrots as they could do; if sown now they will yield a large return. Mangolds and *kohl rabi* should also be sown now.

In the FRUIT GARDEN, the busy season for transplanting is at hand. It is most important that this should be done early in the season, as a young growth is thus started and the tree is somewhat established before the cold winds of winter set in. If previous reminders have been heeded, all new orchard ground should be now ready, having been turned up and exposed to the ameliorating influence of the summer sun for some weeks back. Deciduous trees can be left till next month, but all the orange tribe and evergreens, such as olives, flacourtia, loquat, guava, custard-apple, &c., are better put out now. Do not plant too deep; the nearer to or even on the surface, if such has been duly prepared, the better, and the earth required can be shovelled from the intervening spaces in order to cover the roots. All evergreens may be secured by wire to three stakes driven down not close to the trunk, but some 2 feet away and equi-distant from each other; taking the precaution to put a bit of bagging or rag to prevent the wire from injuring the bark. Do not forget to mulch thickly, and water plentifully immediately the transplanting is done; a day's neglect of this precaution may cause the failure of the tree if the weather should prove hot.

In the VEGETABLE GARDEN, the full season for cool-weather plants is at hand. Hoeing does much to help all growing plants. Sowings should now be made of peas; by putting in different kinds a succession of gatherings can be got. The Chinamen stick to the Yorkshire Hero all through the year and it is a grand sort; but it is better when ordering from the seedman to tell him to assort your order—giving early and late kinds. Carrots, parsnips, beet, turnips, cabbage, cauliflower, lettuce, radish, and mustard and cress can be sown. For broad beans this is a good time; they want moisture, and the land should be in good heart; when the trouble is taken to peel off the outer skin after they are shelled, except when very young, they are much more palatable; around Brisbane and on the Downs they are most productive. Herbs can now be sown, in drills of course, so that they can be weeded and afterwards transplanted; about half an inch is a good depth for such seeds, and the precaution to press some fine earth firmly against the seed should not be neglected; also shade and keep fairly, but not too, moist. This is a very good way for the cottager to get a home collection of herbs for kitchen use, for sage, marjoram, thyme, balm, rue, rosemary, carraway, &c., can thus be raised. Mint is most readily increased by dividing the old roots. Onions can be sown and also transplanted, and so can eschalots. Early celery should now be earthed up; do this carefully so as not to let the soil fall between the leaves. The best plan is, after the earth has been drawn up to the plant by the hoe, to further draw it close around each individual with one hand, grasping the leaves with the other, 5 inches or 6 inches of top being left uncovered. This should be repeated as growth goes on. The giant varieties of celery are now seldom used, the dwarfs being preferable on account of their requiring much less labour, and being more solid and sweet. Attend constantly to weeding and cleanliness.

In the FLOWER GARDEN, annuals suitable to a cooler clime can be sown now, such as nemophilas, Virginian-stock, mignonette, escholtzia, lupins, sweet-william, &c. It is better to sow under a slight shade and always in drills; do not sow too deeply, and press the earth down firmly on the lightly-covered seed with a brick. Cuttings of all kinds of plants that can thus be propagated can now be taken. Bedding plants, such as pelargoniums, verbenas, petunias, gaillardias, if trimmed now, will soon bloom again. Transplant successions of *phlox Drummondii* for winter flowering, and any other hardy annuals in the seed-beds can also be put out; a single plant in each place is better than more. Bulbs of all sorts should be planted. Evergreen shrubs and ornamental trees should now be transplanted, as also can any herbaceous plants. Dahlias that are past their bloom should be lifted by passing a spade under them and working it gently upwards; this causes the plant to wither and the tubers to ripen, and in the course of a fortnight they can be lifted and stored. Any young seedling hollyhocks should be transplanted now; they will do much better than if left till the spring.

In the BUSH-HOUSE, look carefully after pots of seedlings, such as cinerarias, calceolarias, and primulas, and while keeping them in a cool place, put them as near the light as possible, or they will become drawn and weakly. As soon as the seeds are well up and the plants strong, begin to shift the sheets of glass a little at a time to harden the young plants by degrees, and as soon as you can, give them the benefit of light and air. Encourage fuchsias to make growth by repotting into rich compost and watering them. Keep a good supply of rich compost always ready for potting, and wash all used pots. Boxes of violets and pansies will be a good addition to the bush-house in winter. Continue to propagate all useful soft-wooded plants, and pot off such as are wanted at once. Look after ferns, and make renewals where necessary. Lighten the shade if it is anywhere too dense.

MAY.

In the FIELD, late crops of maize will be maturing and should be harvested as soon as ready. For fodder purposes maize may still be sown, but only in very exceptional cases can a crop of corn be reckoned upon. English potatoes may still be planted in warm and sheltered situations. Early-planted ones should be kept well earthed up and thoroughly clean. Oats, barley, and rye may be sown still for green fodder or haymaking purposes; and this month is found to be a good one for sowing wheat. Sow thinly—about a bushel or a bushel and a quarter to the acre—and when about 6 inches high turn in sheep to eat it off, and you will find the wheat plants will tiller and give as heavy or a heavier crop than if sown more thickly. Lucerne may still be sown if suitable land, clean and well prepared, is ready for it. We repeat what we have often said before—no crop is of more, if even equal service to the cultivator or cattle-owner than lucerne. By all means endeavour to get in a plot of lucerne. Mangel-wurzel, swede turnips, *kohl rabi*, carrots, and root crops generally, may still be sown. These are all extremely serviceable for feeding stock, and if sown timely will be ready for use when the supply of the natural grasses fails. The great advantage root crops offer to the stock-owner is that they grow well when the native grasses are at a standstill, and on the other hand cease growing when the heat is sufficient to make the grass grow. Cabbages are useful in the same way and for the same reasons, for they only grow well when a low temperature prevails. Sorghum, imphee, Egyptian corn, and millet, may still be sown, and early-sown fodder crops will now be coming on for immediate use. Any of these fodder plants or *setaria Germanica* will suit for Northern cultivation at any time during winter. Look after late-planted cane and see that the young shoots are well protected from cold or frost, but do not earth them up; let the entire surface of the plantation be level when the work is done. Take every opportunity of using the cultivator amongst growing crops, for it will increase the crop and help to enrich the land at the same time.

In the KITCHEN GARDEN, a good supply of winter vegetables should now be in a forward state, and should be encouraged to develop themselves faster by frequent stirrings of the surface. Earth up early plantings of cabbages and cauliflowers, and also of English potatoes. Plant out cabbages and a few cauliflowers, and sow seeds of both to keep up a succession, but it is almost late for cauliflowers to succeed unless in very rich, deep, and well-worked soil. English potatoes may still be put in where the situation is warm and sheltered from frost. Peas and broad beans may be sown, and if the weather is dry, steep the seed in tepid water for about twenty-four hours before sowing it. Sow full crops of carrots, parsnips, beets, turnips, kohl rabi, and salsify, and continue to sow a small quantity of radishes, lettuces, cress, and salads generally, to keep up a succession. Make plantations of asparagus and rhubarb, and for the latter make provision for artificial shading through the summer; but whatever you do, don't interpret "artificial shading" to mean under living trees. Most plants which need shade would yield as well in the fire as under the shade of a living tree, for the tree roots would kill them. Leave no vacant spot in the garden to run wild, but as soon as one crop is out of the ground break up the land roughly in readiness for the next. By this means you assist Nature to fertilise the soil, and weeds are kept in check. Rosellas begin to ripen this month, and where they are in sufficient quantity may be gathered and dried for use the whole summer through. The drying is easily done by spreading them in the sun on sheets of iron or zinc; or if these are not to be had conveniently, by spreading them on calico.

In the FRUIT GARDEN, preparations should now be in perfect readiness for the reception of any trees required. Planting may be delayed for a few weeks, but in the majority of cases oranges, citrons, and such like, are better put in this month, or early in the next, than later. Beware of purchasing orange trees worked on the lemon stock, for they are a failure everywhere in Queensland, and the direct cause of most of the failures with which our orange growers are troubled. Orange trees worked on the lemon stock are dear at a gift. The pruning of evergreen fruit trees should be attended to as the wood ripens and the crop is gathered. Deciduous trees should be left until the leaves have fallen, both for planting and pruning. Whatever trees are planted be sure that the top is cut back to match the roots, so that both may stand a chance and start together. When the top is left on and little root below, the roots have all, or more than they are able to do to fill the wood with sap, and leaves are of slow development; the plant therefore labours under excessive disadvantages in its endeavour to perform its functions, and the consequence is it either barely exists for many months or even years, and in a dry season, being weak and exhausted, succumbs altogether. This is the brief history of many a failure in planting an orchard. The only safe and sure way is to use the knife freely; you will be in every way the gainer by doing so. Plant your tree carefully after pruning it, and if the stem is at all long and weak secure it firmly to a stake as long as itself. While pruning your trees take notice whether they have stood long there and need manure, if so treat them with a liberal supply, and they will " return the compliment." Keep all orchard land free of undergrowth of any kind. Whatever other and moister climes may be capable of, Queensland has not a sufficiently regular supply of moisture to allow trees to do any good and carry grass or anything else besides. Every inch of land in this climate should be well and deeply worked, and the surface always kept clean and open, for a crop of fruit worth anything to be gathered. It is a fatal mistake to attempt otherwise.

The FLOWER GARDEN, should now begin to be gay with roses and choice flowering plants and many English annuals, and with a little constant care and attention may be kept so for the whole of the winter and spring. If annuals have not been sown lose no time in putting them in, and to make up in a measure for lost time give the soil a little extra top-dressing with some well decomposed fertiliser. Choose showery weather for sowing the seeds, and if you make a constant practice of mulching all the seeds sown you will prevent many a failure. Before the month is out you may commence filling up vacancies with roses and ornamental shrubs, such as poincianas, lagerstremias, jacarandas, magnolias, camellias, azaleas, and such like. The two last-named and also crotons can be made to weather the seasons in Queensland by artificial shading the first year after planting, beginning from now. The soil requires to be deeply worked, thoroughly pulverised, and well firmed with the foot around these latter plants when they are planted, to give them a fair chance to become established, and afterwards they must be regularly watched for signs of failing moisture, or they quickly die from drought. Towards the end of the month prune your roses, and in a shady bed plant the cuttings. You may do the same also with any favourite shrub you may wish to increase.

In the BUSH-HOUSE, relieve the inmates of any excess of shade and give them all the light and air you can. Start geraniums, fuchsias, begonias, and roses into fresh growth when they have had a rest, so as to give bloom in winter and early spring, and to be in readiness for floral exhibitions. Look after seedlings, such as pansies, cinerarias, gloxinias, petunias, geraniums, primulas, and the like, and see that they have plenty of food, moisture, light, and air, and all of them can be made to give fairly satisfactory returns. Replenish the fernery where necessary, and take every opportunity of renewing your compost heap by saving all vegetable matter and giving it a corner to decompose in; and by keeping a supply of clean sand and friable mould, with well decomposed manure to make it with. Re-pot old and resting plants into fresh soil, cutting them back when doing it; this will renovate and revive them. In planting choice plants out into the open ground always give them sufficient rich compost to make them start into vigorous growth.

JUNE.

In the FIELD, cereals, such as oats and wheat, may still be sown. In rich land barley may be put in, but as a rule it is not so hardy or reliable for a fodder crop as oats; some farmers who have tried wheat give it the preference in this climate for making into hay before oats or barley, simply because it will withstand the drought better—no small consideration. Experienced farmers strongly recommend the steeping of seed-wheat in brine and drying it with lime as a preventive to those dread scourges—smut and rust; and experiments made expressly to test the value of the operation speak well for it. Lucerne may be sown yet if land is sufficiently moist, but without rain to give the seed a fair start it is best left alone. It is essential for success with this fodder plant that a good clean seed-bed be prepared for it, otherwise failure may safely be calculated on. Broadcast sowing has its advocates everywhere, but only with the cleanest of land which has received the best of cultivation is it worth while to try it. Our colonial farmers have not yet shown sufficient thoroughness in their work to be safe with broadcast sowing; in most cases the result would be a crop of weeds only fit for ploughing under. From 15 inches to 18 inches apart drills should be made and the seed sown, and as soon as it is above ground and can be seen, the horse-hoe or scarifier should be set to work between the drills to destroy all weeds. Early planted English potatoes will now be forward, and when frost appears it would be well for all hands to go over them early in the morning and brush the hoar frost off with boughs. It is an effectual check to much of the mischief occasioned by frost. Mangel-wurzel, swede turnips, kohl rabi, and carrots may still be sown; stock enjoy and thrive upon them immensely, and they will grow when grass cannot. Sow also cabbage. Those who have a good plot of sweet potatoes will find the value of them in winter, for nothing surpasses them for feeding stock, and more especially for milch cows. It is simply a mistake to lift sweet potatoes; for when lifted they do not keep. They are seldom anything the worse for leaving in the ground so long as the tubers are not exposed to the frost, and it would be well to earth them up a little where such is the case, or cover them with long litter of some kind. Where bandicoots are troublesome, pound up sweet potatoes with arsenic and lay baits for them, or if their runs can be made out they can in some instances be snared. See that all late planted cane is sufficiently covered with earth not to be cut off with frost. This is the best time in the year for clearing and breaking up new land, and where cane planting is intended in the spring the land should now be made ready for it. Plough deep and sub-soil too, and when the land has enjoyed sufficient fallow to mellow it, run the plough through it the second time, and by rolling and harrowing contrive to bring it into a good state of tilth. Tobacco will now be done with for the season and should be cleared off, manure spread upon the land, and a deep ploughing follow it immediately; the rougher the land is left in the meanwhile the better. Land intended for tobacco must be rich or in good heart. Let all unoccupied land be treated similarly, for if no other good comes of it fewer insect pests will live. Keep all growing crops clean and the surface loose and light.

In the KITCHEN GARDEN, many vegetables should be at their best, and with clean cultivation and occasional stirrings of the soil will continue to grow. As crops are removed break up the land afresh; and where necessary apply some good fertiliser. Good vegetables cannot be had without plenty of manure of some kind, but what the fertiliser shall be, circumstances must dictate. Nothing is better than partially decomposed stable manure, if that can be had; bone dust is also a reliable fertiliser. Cabbage plants, if available, may be planted out in showery weather, or, with a little shading furnished by a leafy twig or two around a plant, and artificial watering, they may be planted out at any time. Don't try cauliflowers, except in the Southern and Western districts, for it is late. Sow peas and broad beans, soaking the seeds twenty-four hours before putting them out. Sow all kinds of salads in deep mellow soil. Sow also carrots, turnips, parsnips, beetroot, onions, leeks, and herb seeds. Divide and transplant sage, mint, thyme, marjoram, and all kinds of pot and medicinal herbs. Eschalots and potato-onions should be divided and replanted this month or not later than next. Make asparagus and rhubarb beds; trench and manure well for them, and for the latter provide shade during the summer. Break up any new land, and leave it as rough as possible for the elements to mellow it. Melons, cucumbers, and plants of that class, like virgin soil best so long as it is sufficiently rich, and land broken up now will be nicely ready for them in the spring. Give all weeds short shrift.

In the FRUIT GARDEN, push forward all planting operations. "Hasten slowly" is the motto. Do your planting promptly and seasonably, but do it well. The land for planting should be ready, and proceed at once to place its future occupants. The best plan is to mark out your land, and drive stout stakes firmly into the ground wherever a tree is to be put; then open around the stake and plant to it, tying the tree securely thereto when planted. By driving the stakes first the roots sustain no injury from the operation. Start pruning; first with evergreens, thinning out where too close, and shortening where weak and straggling. Prune deciduous trees when they have cast their leaf. Leave the vines until the end of the month, and then select good strong young shoots for cuttings. Look after strawberry beds, and cut clean away everything but the plants in rows. Top-dress with manure and fork it in, and then strew the surface with good clean straw or grass for mulch. Gather all fruit as it ripens and store it in a cool dry place or market it at once. Attend to all blighted and diseased trees, and give them a dressing; or if the trees have been fairly tried and proved incorrigible, uproot them and find substitutes. Some trees are like animals and men, and have naturally weak constitutions; if so, they are more bother than profit, and will always be so. Leave neither grass nor undergrowth of any kind to occupy the land where large trees are growing and fruiting, or you cannot gather anything like a fair crop of fruit even with good weather, and in droughty seasons you will have none. While trees are young a light crop for a year or two does but little harm; still it does a little, for it keeps the trees back in their growth even then.

In the FLOWER GARDEN much may be done, by care and attention, to keep the borders gay. Water occasionally if dry weather prevails, and mulch choice plants wherever it can be done conveniently. Mulch and hide it if appearances are against it, but mulching is too valuable an aid to successful cultivation in this climate to be kept out of the flower garden. If water is scarce, economise it by plunging a flower pot up to the rim at a sufficient distance from the stem of the plant to prevent the roots from being disturbed, and apply what water you can spare through that. No water is wasted by evaporation when it is applied in that way. Sweet peas, mignonette, larkspurs, candytuft, and many other annuals may still be sown for spring flowering. Plant roses and ornamental shrubs in deeply-worked, well-enriched, and otherwise thoroughly-prepared land. Without thoroughness in cultivation good flowers and plenty of them cannot be had; with it, they may and almost always. Fill up vacancies in the flower borders with choice bedding plants. Plant spring-flowering bulbs, such as oxalis, narcissus, ranunculus, anemone, hyacinth, gladiolus, ixias, babianas, sparaxis, amaryllis, the Mexican tiger-flower, and liliums. Light sandy soil well enriched suits them best. English daisies, violets, and pansies will all be grateful for an occasional good soaking, and especially with weak liquid manure, and will show their gratitude by blooming freely. Plant out rooted layers or piping of pinks, canartions, and picotees. Transplant ten-week and other stocks and all choice annuals when the weather permits. Trim up edgings. Prune roses and evergreens and plant cuttings. Make everything clean and trim. Lift dahlia roots and store them in a cool dry place till spring.

In the BUSH-HOUSE, lighten the shading wherever it is at all dense, or the plants will be too drawn and weakly to bloom well. Without plenty of air and light, good bloom is out of the question. Ferns and foliage plants will do with less light than those which are for bloom. Orchids, again, require strong light to bloom well, and these should become favourites everywhere in Queensland for bush-houses. Early-sown primulas, calceolarias, cinerarias, gloxinias, and cyclamens, will now need all the light they can get, and even a little bottom heat would be helpful to them if it could be had, but that can be done without. Keep them carefully watered, and if they become infested with insects contrive to fumigate them with tobacco smoke, or syringe them with tobacco water. Keep fuchsias growing with weak liquid manure to encourage them to bloom, for the cooler season of the year is when they will show to the best advantage. Strike cuttings of fuchsias, the points of growing shoots being always the best. Discard all old coleus, and see that you have plenty of young plants coming on to supply their places with in the spring. Renew and make ferneries and rockeries. Keep a good supply of well-rotted compost always on hand for potting with ; and plenty of charcoal or broken crocks for drainage. Avoid a live shade for all growing plants, or they cannot thrive and give satisfaction. Water no more than is necessary, especially such plants as coleus, caladiums, and the denizens of warm climes, for they require most water in the warm growing season. Water azaleas and camellias with weak liquid manure about once a week to strengthen the plants and encourage blooming.

JULY.

In the FIELD, preparations should now be pushed forward vigorously for planting early cane. Land which has been under crop for a time, not stumped or ploughed, ought to be taken in hand to have it in readiness, if possible, to plant while the spring thunderstorms are about. Deep ploughing should in all cases be regarded as essential, and every possible way of keeping the land in good heart from the commencement should be devised and persistently carried out. The consequences of not doing so are now manifest in all the older plantations. Cane will now be ripening; any appearing backward may be assisted by trashing. A full crop of English potatoes may be planted this month, but as early in it as possible. The early crop will be ripe and ready to lift, if not already lifted. Plant deep, more especially in light soils, and plant only such seed as shows a readiness to start into growth at once. It is little or no use to plant again the tubers just harvested, for they will not start to grow for a long time, and will then, in all probability, come away irregularly. This applies with special force within the tropics, and it is almost, or quite, too late to put them in here. New Zealand, Tasmanian, or Victorian seed potatoes will serve best. Wheat may still be sown, and, if the season continues favourable, with excellent prospects of doing well. Oats may still be sown, either for fodder, green or dry, or for grain. Lucerne may be tried also, if moisture continues plentiful. While lifting the sweet potato crop select all the small tubers useless for domestic purposes, and reserve them for planting. Don't keep them long out of the ground, but when you have enough to serve for a planting put them in the same distances apart as cuttings in the summer; by so doing you may have sweet potatoes for use in early summer. Generally speaking, the small tubers grow into very large ones, and other smaller ones form at the root besides. Mangel-wurzels, carrots, and swede turnips may still be sown for feeding to stock during spring and early summer. In warm and sheltered localities an early crop of maize may be sown towards the end of the month. In the tropical North the present month should be the best in all the year for maize, if the moisture is sufficient. If the season continues moist enough a sowing of rice may be made late in this month or early in the next. Tobacco should be sown in July, for transplanting during the thunderstorms of September. Arrowroot is now ready for lifting and preparing, and during the winter months the tubers yield more starch and of a better quality than when the weather gets warm. Cotton and coffee may both be sown by the end of the month. Sorghum, imphee, and millet, will also do to go in before the month is out, if the weather is favourable. Keep the horse-hoe and cultivator going during dry weather amongst growing crops. In the North teosinte or *Setaria germanica* may now be sown if the season is moist, and both are very excellent fodder plants.

In the KITCHEN GARDEN, much may yet be done to prolong the season of vegetables. A last sowing of cabbage may be made, and the most reliable kinds to sow are such as are aphis-proof. St. John's Day is about the best for summer use, and Baxter's aphis-proof cabbage should be another, but the former variety is proved most reliable. In the North it is now too late for sowing cabbage seed. Another sowing of peas may be made, and if two or three varieties which will make a succession be put in simultaneously, so much the better. A few French beans may be sown early in the month and towards the close a full sowing. Radishes and lettuces may still be sown, and growing crops of these and salads generally should be copiously watered to bring them on quickly, and make them crisp and sweet. Early sown watercress will now be growing, and will need daily watering to bring it on quickly. Shading from the sun, without excluding the light, will tend to make it more tender and sweet. Plant English potatoes, following advice given above for field planting; and the same with reference to sweet potatoes. Beetroot, carrots, and onions may be sown, and in low moist land also parsnips; the latter root, however, does much better when having the whole winter to grow in. Divide pot herbs and eschallots; also sow seeds of the former. Towards the end of the month a few rows of white or sweet maize may be sown, for use as a vegetable, as an excellent substitute for green peas. In the North this should be largely grown at this season and all through the winter, as it would thrive better than peas, and is a good substitute. In warm and sheltered localities pumpkins, vegetable marrows, cucumbers, and melons may be sown. Everywhere north of Mackay all these, and in fact most vegetables, are only thrifty during the cooler months of the year. Make a point of removing all spent crops to the compost heap, and immediately breaking up the land ; if not wanted at once let it be left in the rough. Keep all growing crops clean from weeds, and the surface soil open and light.

In the FRUIT GARDEN, all planting and pruning operations should be prosecuted with promptitude and vigour, for both should be finished by the end of the month. Look over all the fruit-trees carefully for signs of disease or blight, and while giving them their annual pruning it will be well to give them also a good washing to exterminate insect pests. Soft soap and sulphur are found to be excellent remedies mixed in equal proportions—say a tablespoonful of each to a gallon of water, boiling the water until the ingredients are thoroughly dissolved. The best way to apply it is by means of a moderately fine rose of a patent brass syringe, an indispensable implement to the orchardist. A good syringing with water very hot and near boiling—say 180 degrees Fahr.— is also very efficacious ; or an equally efficacious remedy is supplied by James Pottie, of Sydney, in the shape of a soluble kerosene. See that your trellises for vines and passion fruits are good and sound, and a vigorous pruning to the latter plants will be beneficial to the coming crop. Prune coffee trees, cutting out all the inner growth and suckers, leaving them open enough for the hand to pass freely among the branches, and when the shrubs are about 4 feet 6 inches high stop their upward growth, for the greater convenience of gathering the crop. Mulch the strawberry beds with clean grass or straw, and give the plants a copious watering occasionally when they start to flower. If a cool shady border can be found, or be made artificially, plant a few rhubarb roots. Follow up the advice given on former occasions in keeping all fruit lands clean and free from undergrowth, such as grass or weeds ; let them have as clean cultivation as a bed of cabbage, if you wish good and satisfactory returns. In the North all kinds of tropical trees should be planted now, and while the trees are young and tender they should be shaded with boughs from the direct rays of the sun, and the surface of the soil mulched.

In the FLOWER GARDEN, a good display of bloom will now be making if previous reminders have been duly attended to. English annuals will be fast coming into blossom, and roses also gay with their sweet flowers, if seasonable attentions have been bestowed upon them. Finish all pruning as early in the month as possible, and anything you require to propagate you may strike from cuttings planted thickly in a shaded and well-prepared bed. Many good bedding plants, such as geraniums, double petunias, and heliotropes, may be struck from cuttings planted in the open borders, if put into deeply worked and otherwise suitable soil out of the reach of tree roots. Never expect to strike cuttings under the shade of growing shrubs, or you will be disappointed. Shade is good, but a living shade is injurious. Even pot plants cannot thrive under the shade of growing trees, much less anything in the soil. Towards the end of the month summer flowering annuals, such as balsams, cockscombs, amaranths, portulacas, and zinnias, may be sown; also seeds of verbenas and geraniums. Plant bulbs of gladiolus, sparaxis, and other of the Cape varieties; also bulbs of the hippeastrum and amaryllis. Stake and tie all straggling plants, or cut them back trim and neat; for an untidy flower garden, however gay with blossom, is an eyesore. Finish planting roses and evergreens. Plant camellias and make a shade over and around them, to stand throughout the first year, or they may not survive the summer; the second year they probably will do without it, and be all right if not too crowded with other plants. Overcrowding is certain death to tender things in hot and dry weather. Thin out annuals to only a plant or two in a place, and use those lifted for filling in vacancies elsewhere. Trim and plant edgings, and study cleanliness and neatness everywhere.

In the BUSH-HOUSE, follow up the directions of previous months in keeping the shade just sufficient, thinner than in summer, and only the shade of dead boughs at that. For ferns this advice may be disregarded, but for nothing else. Encourage fuchsias, cinerarias, cyclamens, primulas, and so forth, to push vigorously and bloom early, by frequent attentions, necessary waterings, and an occasional supply of weak liquid manure. Pot off young plants of coleus for summer growth into small pots, and if cold weather prevails plunge the pots up to their rims in sawdust or something of the kind to keep the cold from their roots, and stand them in a cold frame, if such is available. Pot off young fuchsias with rich compost, and encourage them to make wood. Make up ferneries. Keep a supply of compost ready for potting, but not in a dry place; it should always be kept moist. If worms are in the pots submerge them for a while in strong lime water. The present season of the year is the best for making bush-houses, and the early months of spring are the best for planting, renewing, or renovating them.

AUGUST.

In the FIELD, English potatoes may be planted now with a good prospect of success, but as a rule they do not crop well north of the tropic of Capricorn at this season of the year. Small tubers of the sweet potato planted now will give a good crop about Christmas. Small tubers invariably grow into large potatoes, and give a good increase besides, and an abundance of tops for either planting or cattle-feeding. Sorghum and imphee may be sown now, either in drills 3 feet apart or thickly in a bed, to be afterwards transplanted. If plenty of moisture be in the ground it would be well to make a sowing of lucerne, although it is late, March being the best month for it. Tobacco ought to be put in at once if not already done. It should be sown in a bed thoroughly enriched and pulverised—an ounce of seed being sufficient to furnish plants for an acre of land. A very good plan in sowing tobacco is to cover the bed when roughly dug with small boughs thickly enough to make a good fire and leave a good top-dressing of ashes; and when the fire is out prepare the surface and sow the seed, watering and coating it with a light fine mulch. Arrowroot, yams, and tapioca should be planted. A full crop of maize may be sown to advantage this month, especially in warm and sheltered situations; in the extreme North it is quite late enough, and should not be delayed. Intending planters of sugar-cane should have their land in readiness for putting it in. Cuttings should have from three to four eyes; any more are no advantage. In fact, if there is any scarcity of material for planting, cuttings may be prepared of one eye or bud only, and in the majority of cases these single buds produce as strong a stool as when the cuttings are longer. In planting make holes from 8 inches to 10 inches deep, and lay the cutting in a horizontal position at the bottom, with the upper end an inch or so higher than the other, and the buds on either side of the cutting. Cover with about an inch of soil, and afterwards as it advances add more earth until the surface is level, but never earth it up, as it encourages the stool to become too shallow-rooted. Keep all growing crops clean. In strong soils in the cooler portions of the colony a good area of field peas may be sown with a fair prospect of a crop. In suitable land rice may now be sown; ti-tree swamps are very suitable for this crop, and it can either be used for fodder or grain. The present month is as good as any for sowing Egyptian corn; it should be sown much the same as sorghum or imphee. Seeds of ever-green millet and Johnson grass should be sown now; and that the seed may have every chance to germinate, it should be drilled in and firmed well with the foot afterwards. In the extreme North, téosinte and *Setaria germanica* seed should be sown now for use as fodder; the former as far apart as maize, or even 6 feet every way from plant to plant, and the latter like oats or cereals generally.

In the ORCHARD, much pruning and planting generally requires to be done this month; in such cases no further delay should be permitted, as both operations are, when late, attended with much risk. Where planting must be done, do it with extra care, firming the fine soil well to the roots with the foot, and do not forget to mulch and water every tree as soon as it is put in, that is if dry weather prevails. Deciduous trees are now starting into growth, and consequently, if pruned must bleed. If they have not been pruned earlier, and badly need it, proceed with caution and thin out superfluous wood a little, but if pruning can be dispensed with in such cases, by all means leave it undone. Grafting will need attention near the end of this month. Prepare some clay for covering the graft by beating up a mixture of half clay and half horse or cow dung. In this colony all grafting should be done close enough to the ground to be earthed up, or the scion quickly dries and dies through exposure to the sun and drying winds. Vines are now ready to break, and should be tied in to the trellis and the soil lightly forked about them. If not already done, vine cuttings may still be planted. The best cuttings are pieces of last year's wood in lengths of four or five eyes each, or if longer they are none the worse so long as they are inserted deep enough in the soil to cover every bud but the top one. Trenching at least 2 feet deep is a *sine quâ non* to successful grape culture. An orchard filled with large and bearing trees should be well manured and lightly forked, leaving the surface in as rough a state as possible, and on no account should grass be grown on the land. In the extreme North prepare for planting tropical fruits by trenching, manuring, and draining. The greater the soil heat the more imperative does draining become; for the superfluous moisture kills more quickly with great heat than with severe cold. Wait for a plentiful supply of moisture in the ground before planting the trees; but have the ground in readiness now, and a few months to sweeten and pulverise the soil will be of immense advantage to the young roots when planted.

In the KITCHEN GARDEN, the principal work will be attending to growing crops. Peas and beans while young should be kept earthed up; cabbages and cauliflowers also. A good bed of St. John's Day cabbage should be planted now to stand for summer use. An excellent method for growing summer crops of cabbage is to drop a few seeds in a place where the plants are to remain, and thin them out to one afterwards, not transplanting them. By this means they will tend to root deeper, and reach a cooler soil, without which they will not make much growth; for success to be realised, manure should be put down as deeply as possible. Carrots, turnips, beet, and radishes, may still be sown. Celery should be carefully earthed in dry weather; some growers say it is best when not earthed until it has almost made its growth. French beans may now be sown, and also some of the long China runners and the Fijian beans. During the month sow a full crop of pumpkins, cucumbers, melons, and marrows. It may be necessary in the cooler districts to give the young plants a little protection for a few weeks after they show, but it is much better to do that and secure an early crop. Cucumbers and watermelons like plenty of manure and cannot be treated too liberally ; not so pumpkins or marrows. A few rows of some good white Indian corn, such as the Tuscarora, or, better still, a few rows of some sweet corn, should be sown to take the place of green peas for table use. Keep the hoe going freely in dry weather, and mulch and water when necessary. Prepare all vacant plots of land for summer planting, by stirring it deeply and well manuring.

The FLOWER GARDEN should now be a picture with roses and English annuals which succeed here. Pruning and planting of ornamental trees and flowering shrubs should now be over, except such as have been for some time previously growing in pots, otherwise it is getting late for successful transplanting. Recently-planted roses and shrubs should be watered occasionally, should the weather be dry—say once a week—and let it be done thoroughly or not at all. A good covering of mulch around the roots is more helpful in establishing newly-planted things than most of the watering usually done. Seeds of balsam, cockscomb, helianthus, petunia, helichrysum, amaranthus, portulaca, and French and African marigold, may now be sown, and should dry weather prevail an occasional watering will be necessary to make them germinate. Plant out bulbs of gladiolus, sparaxis, ixia, amaryllis, and tuberose, in the cooler parts of the colony; in the tropics they should all be blooming now or nearly so. The last-named are better for lifting occasionally and thinning, as when they increase too much they make but little display. Cut back all overgrown and straggling plants of heliotrope, petunia, geranium, verbena, &c., but in doing so beware of cutting too close, or in this climate and particularly in dry weather they often refuse to start again. Study above all things to have the paths and all the surroundings of the flower garden clean and neat. In shade, with a little regular attention, cuttings of many things may still be struck, but do not make a cutting bed under any living shade, for such is labour and everything else thrown away. As a rule, in sowing seeds have some good compost ready to enrich the spot, so as to give the young plants a vigorous start; for a good beginning will the better ensure a good ending. Watch closely for the beginning of evil in the matter of weeds, for those who weed timely weed well, and will need to do but little.

In the BUSH-HOUSE, let the plants have all the light and heat possible, as many flowering plants will now feel the influence of the spring, which should in every way be encouraged. Too much shade causes a weak growth, and draws the plants so that they have not vigour enough to bloom. Above all, see to it that no living shade is over them, for they will do better without any shade than under a living one. In the case of flowering plants let them in particular enjoy the light, and keep them neat and trim by cutting them in, or by securing to neat stakes properly hidden all straggling growth. In quiet nooks of the bush-house, where light and air circulate freely violets and pansies will succeed, but to secure them, seeds or roots must be had and put out during the autumn. Cinerarias and primulas should be forward enough now to be showing for bloom, and require the sun's influence to hurry them forward. As the former are much preyed upon by caterpillars a little vinegar and water sprinkled upon them will be advantageous. The fernery may still be replenished with young plants of choice varieties, and all decayed and unsightly fronds should be removed with a sharp knife. In the shade of this retreat ferns may be raised from seed (spores) by sowing them on the surface of some good compost in a seed-pan, watering them well and regularly with a very fine rose, and covering the pan with glass to prevent the surface drying; or, better still, sowing them on the peaty clumps of dead stag-horn or elk-horn ferns that are to be had in many places. Young plants of coleus and begonia may be transplanted into larger pots now to be in readiness for a summer display. If fuchsias are not in flower give them the warmest place to bring them forward. Seeds of balsams and cockscombs may be sown now for

K

summer flowering. Finish repotting all large plants such as crotons, dracænas, and marantas, and start caladiums in fresh soil for summer display. In the far North a bush-house should form the principal feature of a well-ordered garden, for it could easily be made exceedingly attractive with orchids, ferns, and such like plants, arranged harmoniously and with taste, and would besides form a cool retreat for personal rest and enjoyment from the sun's fervour. The spring is the best time in the year for the formation and planting of these desirable structures.

SEPTEMBER.

In the FIELD, should rain set in, the spring season will now be opening for summer crops. Maize can be planted in all parts of the colony, and those who in the Southern districts purpose trying cotton should sow now. Continue to set out tobacco plants for a full crop. Plant arrowroot, and the purple variety by preference; few growers who manufacture for sale now plant the white sort, as the purple in this country yields by far the most flour. Plant out the full crop of sweet potatoes as soon as vines can be obtained, and it is worth while using an extra effort to obtain early plants for this very valuable crop. On the Darling Downs and in cool districts English potatoes may be planted early in the month. Cane-planting commences early in September in the Northern districts; in the South the end of the month is considered quite early enough; and many growers prefer to wait for decided spring weather and the warmer soil of October; but a good deal depends upon the season and the rainfall. Concerning the best sorts of cane for various districts, now is the time for planters to see which varieties are turning out best upon soil similar to their own; too much care cannot be devoted to the selection of cane-plants, and there is no advice equal to personal inspection. Arrowroot-making should be pushed ahead, as the bulbs deteriorate in quality after warm growing weather sets in. For spring and summer feed, green corn, téosinte, sorghum, millet, &c., may be sown; the time is also suitable for lucerne and prairie grass, if the soil is in condition and sufficiently moist to start the plants, but usually and in dry weather the season is rather far advanced. Where the wheat crops are heavy, dry weather is very necessary. We are now in the critical time for rust, and when experiments to keep it in check may be put in force. Buckwheat may be sown, and flax where the land is suitable. *Setaria germanica* may now be sown where the soil temperature is about 60 degrees, but the soil should be in a good state of tilth Coffee may be sown this month in beds 3 feet wide, well pulverised and manured; the seed should be put in pretty thickly, and the beds must be watered until the plants appear; as soon as they are fit to handle they should be planted out where they are to remain.

In the FRUIT GARDEN, spring is felt very decidedly, and those who have grafting to do should finish as soon as possible. Transplanting in all branches should also be finished; indeed the time is rather late, even in the cooler districts. As grape vines will now be very forward, use sulphur with them, and freely; it does the young shoots no harm whatever, and may effect much good. Make the young growth of the vines very snug as it becomes lengthy; wind storms during September have proved very destructive by knocking about the young growth of the vines. Trees recently set out should be well supported by stakes, otherwise they also may suffer seriously. Peaches, and other stone fruits, have now set their fruit; and it is very necessary that they be relieved of some of it; otherwise there will be the too common cry of poor fruit—the result, as a rule, of over-bearing. During damp growing weather the peach fly is likely to make its appearance; fires lighted during the evenings attract and destroy the insects, while the smoke aids in driving them off. Other pests of the fruit gardener also develop about this time—amongst them blight, scale, and aphis—on the trees. Alkali washes do good service in driving them off. A sowing of rosella seed may be made, in order to get young plants for setting out as soon as the weather will permit; the rosella, in the Southern districts, requires all the spring and summer growth it can get, and, on its merits, deserves every attention. In the North it is a hardy plant, but sowing should be finished this month, and remember that seed grown in the South will seldom germinate. A coating of mulch will help greatly the germination of the seed. Mulch should also be applied round all newly-planted trees. Now is the proper time to prune peach trees by rubbing off all superfluous and misplaced shoots.

In the KITCHEN GARDEN, planting out cabbage, cauliflower, lettuce, may still be done, but, should the weather set in fine, watering will be necessary. Limited sowings of radish, carrot, turnip, spinach, &c., may be made, but only in well-tilled and manured soil. It is very necessary to keep all the cold weather crops clean and free from weeds after this time; weeds check their growth seriously, and ruin the prospects of a crop. Peas also may be sown under similar conditions, though for them it is rather late; but from this time forward, through the spring and summer, the warm weather crops are the standby of the vegetable garden. Amongst the first of these are cucumbers, the early plants of which can be set out into the open ground as soon as risk from frost is over; and seed sown for succession of plants. Melon seed may be sown in hills where the plants are to grow; all the varieties do well in any moderately rich loose soil. Select a piece of new land for rock melons, which are amongst the finest of the tribe. Sow for Cape gooseberry, capsicum, and tomatoes, as may be required; and all of these fruits do well when young plants are set out. Plant eschalots, artichokes, chives, garlic, &c., and ginger—one of the most deserving of our garden productions; also peanuts. French beans may now be sown as desired, both dwarfs and climbers; they form the backbone of our summer vegetable supply; also the long Chinese runner beans, and the Fiji and Lima beans. A few English potatoes may be sown in the cooler districts; elsewhere it is too late.

In the FLOWER GARDEN AND SHRUBBERY, the transplanted shrubs will now be making signs of growth; they require attention to withstand the effects of wind storms, and also of the weather: for the former there is nothing like snug staking; for the latter, mulching around the newly planted trees is the remedy; it helps to keep the soil loose and prevent it from packing or consolidating. The roses will now be in a fair way for summer growth, but require attention to keep aphis and other vermin in check. Alkali washes are effective for the purpose; where the soil is not sufficiently rich to give full hearty growth, manure may be worked into the surface carefully. Hard-wooded plants, as the magnolia, camellia, gardenia, tea and coffee shrubs, the varieties of hibiscus, &c., can be propagated by layering at this season, or at any time during moist growing weather. Asters, German stocks, and others may be set out, and many annuals sown in any desired quantity and variety; but there ought to be a good show of most of these in bloom by this time. Vacancies, as they occur, may be filled in with coleuses, geraniums, petunias, heliotropes, verbenas, and other useful bedding plants, or with patches of seed, such as balsams, cockscombs, phloxes, portulacas, amaranths, and similar tender annuals. Plant out dahlias, and at the same time drive a good stake down close by the side of the bulb to secure the young and tender shoots to when they begin to push. Or the plan now coming into vogue in the old country, of pegging the shoots down flat over the bed, may be adopted, as being especially suited for the exigencies of our climate.

In the BUSH-HOUSE, as the heat increases, attend to the top shading to see that it is sufficient. Rooted cuttings of coleus saved through the winter may now be planted in pots. Caladiums will now require repotting to encourage good growth. All flowering plants, such as fuchsias, primulas, cinerarias, calceolarias, and the like should be as near the light as possible to prevent their becoming weakly and drawn. Fuchsias should be encouraged to make their best growth and to flower as soon as possible; the same also may be said of begonias. Violets and pansies should have the coolest place that can be found, and remain in it for the summer. The latter may be kept alive through the summer, and be ready to flower early in the autumn, if thus cared for. Repot large ferns, and renew the fernery generally; and, where necessary, replenish the soil with compost adapted for the purpose, which should be composed of leaf mould, sawdust, or decomposed vegetable matter, and a large proportion of sand. Compost for most plants requires to be moderately firm and compact, but at the same time porous and light.

OCTOBER.

In the FIELD, full crops of maize may yet be sown. Deep tillage is a wonderful help to corn crops; and those who have tried the subsoil plough in loosening the under strata and breaking the hard pan formed by the plough in shallow working, have found such great benefit from it that they are not likely to discontinue its use. Oats and lucerne will soon be ready for making into hay, and hay-makers should contrive to have their hay cured without drying it too much and destroying its nutritive properties. Less drying, and the use of salt in stacking it, or of good ventilation into the heart of the stack, would be helpful in producing a more valuable and marketable article. The spring crop of English potatoes should be kept well earthed, and as they ripen no time should be lost in lifting them, as they are much injured by the heat of the soil if left long in the ground. The planting of arrowroot should now be completed as early as possible, for, the growing season having commenced, the tubers should be in to take the full benefit of it. Sweet potatoes may also be planted if cuttings can be obtained, and if not, plant some of the small tubers instead, as they, with good weather, will increase in size, and grow into large potatoes. It is possible in good soil to grow sweet potatoes up to 12 lb. or 14 lb. weight in this way. This is also the proper season of the year to sow cotton. Three or four seeds should be dropped into holes from 3 feet to 5 feet apart; the richer the soil the more room the plants require; and after they come up thin out all but one, of course leaving the strongest. Indigo is another plant of commercial value well suited to this climate, and seed of it should also be sown now. Drills, 12 inches apart, should be opened out about 3 inches deep, and seed sown, always choosing moist warm weather for doing it. The transplanting of tobacco should be continued, and all care in shading and watering taken of the young plants after they are put out. About 4 feet apart each way is the correct thing for tobacco. Cane-planting may now be prosecuted with vigour, for the earlier it is in the longer it has to make its growth, and to mature its crop of plant-cane. When a ratoon crop has been cut and cleared off, the plough should be set to work to stir up the soil, and if previous to so doing some good fertiliser has been applied, the results will certainly be the better for it. Attend to all early sown crops of maize and so forth with the cultivator and scarifier, and see that the crop is not robbed of its substance by a second crop of weeds.

In the KITCHEN GARDEN, give due attention to all early sown spring crops, so that they may have every chance. Stir the soil occasionally between them to keep it light and open and free from weeds. Sow seeds of cucumbers, melons, vegetable marrows, and pumpkins, if not already done, and give them frequent waterings to bring them on. In a cool situation, radishes, lettuces, and cress, may still be sown, but they must be watered regularly to be of any service now that hot weather has set in. In showery weather another planting of cabbages may be made, and great watchfulness will be necessary with this crop to keep it clear of the aphis. Earth up celery. Manure and dig asparagus and rhubarb beds, taking care not to disturb the crowns of the plants. Rhubarb will be much improved by an application of liquid manure about once a-week, and frequent waterings beside. Sow rosellas and okras in beds for transplanting. Thin out all root crops, such as carrots, parsnips, and beet. Sow tomatoes, capsicums, and chillies. A good sowing of French beans and the long Chinese runner bean may now be sown; also a full sowing of Chinese spinach.

In the FRUIT GARDEN, attend to spring pruning, which consists in pinching off with finger and thumb all misplaced and useless wood while tender. Pay special attention to vines in this particular, and shorten the bearing branches at the next leaf beyond the last bunch, to throw all the strength of the plant into the fruit. Look out for the oidium, and apply the sulphur remedy on its first appearance. If fruit-bearing trees received proper attention in pruning and dressing for blight in the winter, they will now be in full vigour; and heavily-bearing trees should have a good coating of mulch over their roots, and a thorough watering at intervals if dry weather prevails. Mulch keeps the roots cool, and is very beneficial to most crops of fruit, even should moist weather prevail. Plantations of pine-apples and bananas may now at any time be made. Mangoes, jack-fruit, and other sub-tropical fruits at all tender to frost, should now be planted; and to get them established mulch them carefully, and water them at intervals sufficiently to keep the ground moist, but not wet.

In the FLOWER GARDEN, roses and many old-country annuals will now be at their best, and, should dry weather set in, water may be used freely upon them to great advantage. Look after choice annuals for their seed, for many of them throw it almost before it ripens. See that all recently planted roses and ornamental shrubs are all right, and keep the mulch to their roots and the watering-can going whenever they are in any danger of becoming dry. Excess of moisture or drought is much more injurious to anything newly planted than after it is established. Fill up vacancies with bedding plants and summer annuals. To obtain seed of good quality persistently remove an inferior plant as soon as its first bloom appears, and leave nothing but the best to bloom, and then you are right. With only one single-stock among a number of good double ones you may rely on getting plenty of double-stocks from the seed, but not so if single-stocks prevail. As spring flowering bulbs die down lift them and store them away in clean dry sand in a cool place. Plant dahlias, and to each root fix a stake to secure the plant to when it starts into growth.

In the BUSH-HOUSE, preparations must now be made for summer, both with reference to the shading and also the inmates. Fuchsias, cinerarias, primulas, and the like are liable to attacks from insect pests, and an excellent preventive is a frequent syringing with clean water, thrown with some force against them on every side. Cyclamens will soon be going out of bloom, and should be then removed to a cool dry place. Keep pansies and violets in a cool corner, but let them have all the light and air you can to prevent them being drawn. Repot begonias, caladiums and young plants of coleus for summer display, and replenish your fernery; also repot large specimens which have occupied their present quarters too long. A peaty soil, or a sandy garden loam mixed with broken cocoanut fibre or refuse, makes a very good potting compost for ferns, mixed freely with broken bricks or potsherds. While providing good shade let light and air have free access, or your chances of success are small.

NOVEMBER.

In the FIELD, harvesting operations are generally in full swing this month, and all the labour available on the farm is absorbed thereby. It is a mistake nevertheless to allow anything to stand in the way of necessary cleaning work among growing crops. A few weeks' neglect will of necessity give as many months' extra work, if it does not altogether do away with the possibility of getting at it at all, and then the crop must suffer. The crops coming on which will need such attentions are cotton, indigo, arrowroot, ginger, yams, recently sown maize, and tobacco. There is nothing better than the horse-hoe or scarifier for such work, and as a rule this implement should be worked between the rows as soon as the plants are large enough to be seen, and before the weeds have made growth, as they are much more easily killed at this stage than at any other, and the stirring helps the crop along the faster. Continue to plant sugar-cane, and draw more earth to newly planted cane as it requires it, ceasing to do it when the land is level. Look after tobacco now advancing in growth; and when it has reached its full height and shows for bloom top it, and at the same time remove all suckers, starting from the stem, and all the lower leaves except the top eight or ten, so that these may receive all the nourishment and strength of the plant. Sow maize, if the weather is favourable, also pumpkins and squashes. Plant sweet potatoes, always choosing "dropping weather" for the operation. Look after early planted English potatoes and lift them at once after they ripen, for they get no good in the hot land. Harvest wheat, oats, and barley, always aiming to cut a week early rather than late, for when left too long the grain wastes in harvesting, and besides, it is not so good or plump. Finish haymaking, and be careful not to overdry it or it is half destroyed.

In the KITCHEN GARDEN, look well after growing crops, keeping them clean, and earth around them light and open. In the Southern districts a few cabbages may still be sown in favourable weather, and the beds should be lightly mulched and regularly watered, or the seeds will neither germinate nor grow afterwards. Look to the tomatoes and put necessary supports to them, or much of the fruit will go to waste on the ground. Thinning them also will be helpful to enlarge the fruit. Seeds of rosellas, cucumbers, rock and water-melons, also vegetable marrows and pumpkins, may still be sown, if not already done. Where asparagus beds have yielded well cease cutting from them or you will weaken them. In the South, French beans may still be sown, but in the Central or Northern districts the heat will, at this season of the year, be getting too much for them. What are called Fiji or Chinese long runner beans may be sown now, and at intervals all through the summer as they are required, and also the variety of spinach grown for market by the Chinese. Make a point of always digging up any vacant bed at once when the crop is off, for in dry weather it will then absorb moisture from the atmosphere, and with that moisture it will also obtain additional fertility; besides, this method is wonderfully helpful in keeping down weeds.

The FRUIT GARDEN requires less attention this month, as the plants are all active. Thin fruit on all trees where it has set too thickly, as it improves the quality without taking much, if anything, from the weight of the crop. Still attend to "finger and thumb" pruning. Watch vines for the oidium, and when needful set to work with the sulphur bellows. Plant pineapples and bananas, for anywhere that they grow at all they will transplant and thrive better when put out in the growing season. Plant out all kinds of tropical fruits, which are mostly grown and sent out in pots. If you have to lift them from the ground, select wet weather for doing it, and take extra precautions in the way of mulching and shading until they are established and make a start. As a rule mulch and shade all newly planted trees or plants, except in continuous wet weather.

In the FLOWER GARDEN, watch for the seeds of annuals now ripening, selecting seed only from such plants as are worthy. As everything will be growing fast now, stake, tie, regulate, and cut away, so that order and neatness may be maintained. Seeds of tender annuals may still be sown as recommended in last month. Bedding plants of suitable varieties may be put out where vacancies occur. Dahlias should be staked, and early flowering spring bulbs lifted and put into a cool shady place and stored in sand until again wanted. Coleus and begonias of some of the hardy varieties may now be put out; and see to them for a while after that they may not perish for want of food and nourishment.

In the BUSH-HOUSE, if the shading has been duly regulated as recommended last month, there should now be a full spring display of blossom—pansies, cinerarias, fuchsias, geraniums, primulas, and, in the cooler districts, probably calceolarias. To keep up a display for the summer much dependence will have to be placed on coleus, caladiums, marantas, begonias, crotons, and other ornamental plants and ferns. Repot young growing plants of coleus and fuchsias, and apply weak liquid manure to flowering plants once a week. In good growing weather renew your fernery, keeping it always well-shaded. There is no better season than this for starting a fernery, as plants put out early in the summer have all the growing season before them, and by the time cool weather sets in they are strong and well-established. Gloxinias and achimenes may be planted out in suitable places in the bush-house to enliven it a little, for they love a little cool shade.

DECEMBER.

In the FIELD, this month a full crop of maize should be sown. This advice applies to the whole of Southern and Central Queensland; farther north it is too late or too early. Earth up and clean all young growing crops of maize. Cleaning operations will occupy much of the time this month if the season is moist, and only dry weather should be chosen for the work. The advice given for last month with tobacco applies equally now, and the first crop should soon be ready for harvesting. Cotton should also be topped and have the superfluous shoots thinned out. Attend to sugar-cane as recommended last month, and continue planting if required and the weather is favourable. Lift English potatoes and store them in a cellar or some cool place; seed should be saved from this crop for March planting. Yams should be staked. Break up ground now or soon for sowing with lucerne in March, as if left in a bare fallow and ploughed again, if weeds appear it may be made tolerably clean before the lucerne is sown—an essential with that crop.

In the KITCHEN GARDEN, but little can be done this month except what was recommended for last. Ground occupied with winter crops should be cleared and dug as they cease doing duty. At intervals of a few weeks sow a few rows of white or sweet corn as a summer substitute for green peas. Water cucumbers, vegetable marrows, celery, and cabbages in dry weather, and while at it do it effectually, for surface sprinklings are absolutely worthless, only a waste of time and water, the heat of the surface soil being so great that it is soon sent away in vapour.

In the FRUIT GARDEN, pinch back the shoots of vines bearing to within a leaf of the last bunch of fruit, and keep them so. Pinch out also all superfluous young wood and do the same with all other fruit trees. The budding of stone fruit—such as peaches—may be commenced towards the end of the month. If not already done attend to the instructions given last month with reference to the planting of tropical fruits.

In the FLOWER GARDEN, the most that can be done now is to keep everything clean and neat, and all straggling plants in their place by pruning or staking. Borders and edgings should be cut at intervals and lawns mowed. The budding of roses may be done at any time now when the bark will run easily. Carnations and picotees may be layered, and also many roses and shrubs. Gather flower seeds as they ripen. Examine bulbs stored away, occasionally, and see that they are perfectly dry and not attacked by mice.

In the BUSH-HOUSE, the directions given for last month are equally available for this. Put all plants, such as cinerarias, pansies, primulas, fuchsias, and the like, into the coolest corner you can find, and plunge them up to the rims in the soil, mulching the soil well afterwards. This will keep their roots as cool as possible, and will probably keep them alive through the summer, and then they will serve you better the following winter and spring. As a rule plunge all pot plants, if possible, through the hottest of the weather, as it saves much labour in watering, and the plants are in every way the better for it.

With reference to the foregoing Calendar it may be taken as suitable for all districts in Queensland where frosts are seldom or never experienced; but on the Darling Downs and all the colder districts of the colony the directions given for February, March and April will in the main be more adapted for July, August and September; most of the directions with reference to the root crops, however, and many of the suggestions given besides, are as suitable for one portion of Queensland as another. Our readers should also exercise what common sense they have in using the calendar, for seasons differ so widely everywhere that general directions can do no more than approximate the truth.

JAMES C. BEAL, Government Printer, William street, Brisbane.

www.ingramcontent.com/pod-product-compliance
Lightning Source LLC
Chambersburg PA
CBHW020054170426
43199CB00009B/283